A SHORT HISTORY

OF THE TWENTIETH CENTURY

A SHORT
HISTORY
OF THE
TWENTIETH
CENTURY

John Lukacs

THE BELKNAP PRESS OF
HARVARD UNIVERSITY PRESS

Cambridge, Massachusetts
London, England
2013

LIBRARY OF CONGRESS CATALOGING-IN-PUBLICATION DATA

Lukacs, John, 1924–

A short history of the twentieth century / John Lukacs.

pages   cm

Includes bibliographical references and index.

ISBN 978-0-674-72536-2 (alk. paper)

1. History, Modern—20th century.   I. Title.

D421.L86   2013

909.82—dc23   2013007948

CONTENTS

A SHORT HISTORY

OF THE TWENTIETH CENTURY

"GOD WRITES STRAIGHT
WITH CROOKED LINES"

"Century"—An American century—The German potentiality—Hitler's primary role—1989 or 1945?—The American
superpower presence—Stalin and the retreat of Russian
power—The end of colonialism—Recovery and rise of
China—The end of the Modern or European Age—From
liberal democracy to the universality of popular sovereignty

THERE IS NO SERIOUS HISTORY of the twentieth century that I
know of; but my purpose in this book is not quite filling that gap.
I lived through much of the twentieth century, and I was a participant in and a historian of a few of its portions. I have devoted
much of my life to asserting, teaching, and writing that "objective" and "scientific" history are inadequate desiderata; but so,
too, is "subjective" history. Our historical knowledge, like nearly
every kind of human knowledge, is personal and participatory,
since the knower and the known, while not identical, are not
and cannot be entirely separate. We do not possess truth completely. Yet pursue truth we must. So many seemingly endless
and incomplete truths about the history of the twentieth century
are still worth pursuing, and perhaps forever.

Now, enough of this philosophic premise. Historical knowledge, nay, understanding, depends on description rather than on definition. It consists of words and sentences that are inseparable from "facts"; they are more than the wrapping of facts. "In the beginning was the Word," and so it will be at the end of the world.

About the term "century": it had none of its present meaning until around 1650, when it appeared in English and French. Before that, it meant a regiment of one hundred soldiers—in Latin, *centuria* (related to the term *centurion,* their commander). That appearance of a new meaning was the mark of an emerging historical consciousness. So was the appearance of words for three historical ages, Ancient, Middle, and Modern. People in the Middle Ages did not know that they were medieval people. They knew that things were changing—some of them for the worse, others for the better—but that was that. *The Waning of the Middle Ages,* written by the great Dutch historian Johan Huizinga, was published in 1920. Five hundred years before, no one, or only a very few, would have understood what that title meant. Our historical consciousness in many ways and forms had progressed by the twentieth century—so much so, that more and more people are somehow aware that we are living during the waning of the Modern Age. Even more obvious is that the twentieth century also meant the end of the European Age: another main theme, or sub-theme, of the present book. Now add to this (historically, not numerically) that the twentieth century was a short century, seventy-five years, extending from 1914 to 1989, marked by two world wars (probably the last), of which the Communist revolution and state in Russia were a consequence; and then that state too collapsed, in 1989. (The historical nineteenth century lasted longer: ninety-nine years, from the fall of Napoleon in 1815 to the outbreak of the First World War in 1914.)

One more matter. The twentieth century was—an? the?—

American century. Such a statement may not surprise many of
my readers; but it would have surprised many of those who lived
before the First, or even the Second, World War. It should not
surprise us to hear or read that 1914–1989 (and now even beyond that) has been an American century, while the nineteenth
was largely a British century and the eighteenth a French one.
These characterizations allude not only to military strength, naval power, and imperial possessions, but to many other kinds
of influences—yet military and naval power mattered above all.
The enormous events of the twentieth century, the two mountain ranges that largely determined its landscape, were the two
world wars—the Second largely a consequence of the First, and
the so-called Cold War almost entirely a consequence of the Second. Without their military alliance with the United States, Britain and Russia, even together, could not have won the Second
World War; without America's entry into the First World War,
the British and French might not have won that either, at least
not in 1918. But there was more to these alliances than military
and sea and air power. They meant the end of the European Age.
A few Europeans had recognized this, looking at the world map
even before 1914: Europe was but a peninsula of Asia.

The British—mostly their successive governments, but also
much of their press—thought they had to have good relations
with the United States, accepting its supremacy in some places
and ways (though seldom admitting this before 1914). As late
as 1895, there was a minor crisis between Washington and London regarding Venezuela. But less than three years later, in 1898,
the American decision to go to war against Spain (a war that
was provoked by the United States) was supported almost without exception by the British government and the British press.
Thereafter, and throughout the twentieth century, there was no

instance in which a British government would strongly oppose the United States. During the fifteen years before 1914, American influence on much of British life grew. Sir James Bryce, who served as ambassador to the United States and knew the country well, went so far as to write (in his book *The American Commonwealth*): "America has in some respects anticipated European nations. She is walking before them along paths which they may probably follow." Much of this went beyond (or beneath) politics. It involved countless examples of American practices and inventions, especially in the English-speaking countries, but also in many other places throughout the world. Even more important: in 1940, Hitler came close to winning the Second World War. Had it not been for Winston Churchill and Franklin Roosevelt, he may have achieved that.

Meanwhile the British presence and influence in the United States were decreasing. Once the British Isles had been the primary source of immigrants to America, but this stream was diminishing in the fifteen years before 1914—a period when immigration from other European countries was still rapidly growing. Theodore Roosevelt, one of America's greatest presidents, was aware of this. His advocacy of a New Nationalism was not nationalism as we understand it today; rather, it was stentorian advice to the new arrivals—at that time coming especially from Eastern and Southern Europe—to become Americanized as soon as they could. This Rooseveltian advocacy was more than successful during most of the twentieth century. Nationalism, of course, has various forms and desiderata, one example of this being the United States of America. Going further, and forecasting one main argument of this book, we can say that nationalism (related to but altogether different from old-fashioned patriotism) has been and still is the most popular and populist political sentiment in the twentieth century, almost everywhere.[1]

"God writes straight with crooked lines": this is a profound and wise Portuguese proverb. Nonbelievers may find this arguable (I do not), but it does not mean that the course of world history was inevitable. Neither was the history of the United States. History does not consist of endless alternatives—but behind or during or prior to every human event, the actuality is colored by a different potentiality. For example, Germany had the potential to become the greatest power in the twentieth century. Toward the end of his life, Hitler once said that he was "Europe's last hope." (Some hope.)[2] Yet he did not really think of himself as a European. (Neither did he quite fathom the great dependence of Britain upon the United States.) Near the end of his life, Otto von Bismarck was reputed to have said that the most important factor in the coming twentieth century would be that Americans spoke English.

Still, there was a possibility that Germany could become a dominant power in the world. There were a few, though not many, Englishmen and Scotsmen advocating for a British alliance with Germany (some of them for racial reasons). There was considerable anti-British sentiment among the American people, and among some of their leaders as well, though it did not amount to much in the long run. But when one contemplates the history of Europe, surely before 1945, many actualities could have been different. The impact and influence of Germany—military

1. There will be extensive reference to this in later chapters.
2. On January 1, 1944, Churchill instructed his three chiefs of staff: "I hope that all expressions such as 'Invasion of Europe' or 'Assault upon the fortress of Europe' may be eliminated henceforward."

as well as political, ideological as well as cultural and intellectual, industrial as well as technological—were still increasing in 1900, in 1914, and even after the First World War, which Germany came close to winning (it came even closer to winning the Second World War, at least from 1939 to 1942). But the First World War was almost exclusively a "European War" (the official name given to it by the British government throughout that war). The Second World War was then fought on other continents and across other oceans; but the inclinations of many Americans notwithstanding, the American military and political leaders were correct in deciding early that the Allies' defeat of Germany must have priority over the American war against Japan that would follow the collapse of Germany. Still, 80 million Germans were ranged against almost 500 million British, Americans, French, and Russians—most decisively in Europe, where it took nearly six years to conquer them.

People in the Far East may argue that the Second World War began not in September 1939 in Poland but in September 1931 in China: in that month, Japanese armies advanced from Manchuria and Korea into China proper, overrunning and occupying its main seaboard cities, penetrating the interior of the country during the next ten years—and eventually leading to war between Japan and the United States. Yet this perspective is insufficient. Japan's ambition to establish its empire along the Far Eastern Asian mainland had existed before 1931. It was also part and parcel of the movement of anticolonialism, arising here and there before 1931. Much of this was also due to the growing evidence of uneasy sentiments among the British and French and also other European nations that were reluctant to extend or even maintain their role in some of their overseas colonies, most of them acquired during the nineteenth century. More important was that in 1939 another war breaking out in Europe was welcomed by the Japanese.

Here I must insist on the obvious. Both world wars broke out in Europe. The events of 1914, the origins of World War I, the cascade of decisions leading to its outbreak, the various parts played by statesmen and by entire governments have been debated among historians for nearly one hundred years, and even now. Yet the outbreak of World War II was due to one man, Adolf Hitler. Had he not started a second world war in 1939, another war in Europe may have come about years later—perhaps. Had he conquered much of Europe, an American-Japanese war may have come about years later—perhaps. Yet "perhaps" and the extent of a potentiality that exists behind actuality are not the same thing.

With the above in mind, let me ask: Was the twentieth century even shorter than I (and presumably others) now see it? Did it end not in 1989 but already in 1945? I wrote that the historical landscape of the twentieth century was dominated by the enormous mountain ranges of the two world wars. Yet after 1945, the age of world wars was over. Such wars may never occur again. There has been, after all, a change in the very structure of international history. The wars after 1945 have been smaller—but their sizes do not matter much. What matters is that they have more often been wars between nations or tribes than wars between states. The existence of nations preceded the formation of states but the former will survive the latter, creating all kinds of problems.

There were other landmark changes in the history of the world after 1945. Almost all wars were now undeclared. Others were fought mainly by air. The United States had become the only superpower in the world. After 1945, most people (and many

Americans) came to think that the political landscape of the world was now marked by two superpowers—one Communist, the other not—wrestling for domination over much of the globe. This was not so. (After General de Gaulle visited the Soviet Union in 1966, he remarked that there was only one superpower in the world: the United States.) But it was not American pressure that led to the dissolution of the Soviet Union. It was the overdue breakup of the Russian Empire, including the ever more obvious nonsense of an international Communism.

Meanwhile, the presence of the United States—perhaps even more than its actual power—grew and grew. The many American military bases around the world shrank in number after 1945, as soldiers were demobilized and sent home, but the Cold War (and other influences) reversed this trend. By 1956 the United States had more than 150 ground, naval, and air bases athwart the globe. That year, the Republican Party's platform cheered them on, calling for an American military presence "all around the world." When the Cold War with the Soviet Union came to its end, there were (and still are) more than 900 such bases. There is reason to think that an American president or even a secretary of defense would not be able to list them all. Oddly enough, only a minuscule portion of the American people have ever been wholly aware of this—unlike substantial portions, probably the majorities, of the British or Dutch or Portuguese or French or Italian people, who a century before had been proud or at least in favor of their country's colonial possessions.

Americans were different. The presence of their bases abroad had little or nothing to do with the natural richness of their colonial possessions, as had been the case with most Europeans. At the same time, most Americans supported the foreign wars that their soldiers fought during the Cold War and after. This was a reasonable choice during the Korean War in 1950–1953, but less so with American military intrusions in the Near East or Vietnam or Iraq; during these involvements, American popular support of costly campaigns waned. A significant symptom of the exceptional nature of the American character was the generous inclination toward recent enemies: the Japanese, Germans, Vietnamese, and so on. Consider, too, the general absence of American self-congratulation when the Soviet Union collapsed, beginning in the 1980s—all of Ronald Reagan's previous bombastic and nationalistic phrases notwithstanding.

That the Second World War did not debouch into another war between the great powers was also due to the—uneasy—acceptance by the Americans, the British, and continental Europeans of the division of Europe in 1945. (This was also due to Stalin and then to his successors, by their calculations.)

It was also the main reason Stalin avoided a war with the United States. He insisted on ruling most of Eastern Europe—no more than that. Russia had an enormous appetite now, Churchill told de Gaulle in November 1944, "but after the meal comes the digestion period," with its many troubles. Near the end of his life, Stalin recognized this. In October 1952, he proposed a settlement involving a reciprocal retreat of Soviet and American forces from an eventually reunited and "neutral" Germany (an American-German alliance was one of Stalin's main fears). He died not long afterward. Soon, Russia began divesting itself of its 1945 conquests. In 1955, it gave up its bases in Austria and Finland (and also its bases in China); it reached a settlement with Yugoslavia. It was stunned and dismayed by the 1956 revolution in Hungary and by the rise of nationalism in Poland. This evolution of a gradual though sometimes interrupted withdrawal of Russian power from Eastern Europe continued until the demise of the Soviet Union in 1989.

Successive American governments and most of the American people were often unwilling to recognize this. In 1959, Nikita Khrushchev, then leader of the Soviet Union, visited the United States to confer with President Dwight Eisenhower. In many ways, he came cap in hand (among other matters, he suggested an American-Russian collaboration against Communist China). The American host—who fourteen years earlier had been one of the more enthusiastic proponents of American friendship with the Soviet Union—received his Russian guest with a sour face and without much interest. By 1952, anti-Communism had become synonymous with American nationalism. An enduring result was the rise of the American "conservative" movement—a political adjective which previously had been unpopular among Americans but which thirty years later many Americans would prefer to "liberal."

Quite different was the history of the so-called Third World (a very imprecise term) after 1945. Opposition to colonialism was an element in the American credo from the country's very beginning. It was a powerful though often indirect factor in the rapid decline of the European Age, as Britain, France, Holland, Belgium, Portugal, and Italy gave up their colonial possessions. So did Japan, of course. Before 1945, almost all of Africa was a European colony of one kind or another. Twenty years later, there were practically no European colonies anywhere in that enormous continent—or in Asia. In the Near East after 1920, the Ottoman Empire gave up just about all of its adjacent possessions inhabited by non-Turkish peoples. Since 1990, such a devolution has been discernible even in some of the older parts of the Soviet Union.

But to declare or regard anti- or noncolonialism as part of a worldwide advance of democracy is misleading. During the Cold War, whether affected by it or not, some places of the world, including states and nations in Central and South America, occasionally installed Communist or pro-Communist regimes. Outside the Russian sphere in Europe (except for Yugoslavia), this did not happen. But Cuba—and later other minor, formerly Spanish colonies—were prime examples of such Communist establishments. Sometimes they absurdly recapitulated the pattern in which revolts against colonialism had occurred long after the conclusion of the French revolutionary and Napoleonic wars, mostly after 1815. Their main purpose was the assertion of national independence, though often their motives were more obscure than that.

In Cuba, the principal motive of Fidel Castro and his supporters (as with those of some other dictators in Central and South America) was not Communism but anti-Americanism. It speaks well of the United States that, save for a few brief, small-scale, clandestine episodes, the American government refrained from subduing these agitated and irresponsible governments militarily. Castro and others soon learned that the help they might expect to get from the Soviet Union was less than minimal. In 1962, when Khrushchev agreed to Castro's frantic requests to furnish Cuba with medium-range rockets (limited in range, and under complete Russian control) against a potential American invasion, a stern American reaction, including a naval blockade, put an end to this largely senseless episode. This Russian presence in the Western Hemisphere faded almost immediately. One of its consequences was the ouster of Khrushchev by his Politburo less than two years later; another was an overall though fitful improvement in American-Soviet relations during the subsequent twenty-five years.

Russia's relations with China were different, as always. China was not one of the great powers of the world in 1945, though President Roosevelt declared that it was. But as so often before, China, despite its enormous size and population, was something like a geopolitical vacuum. The Japanese now left China for good. Within and outside China, the British were likewise packing up. The Chinese government, under Chiang Kai-shek (whose ultimate defeat ought not to obscure some of his merits and political talents), depended largely on the United States. But in and after 1945, Washington and the American military were preoccupied with what to do and where to stand in the Western Pacific, including the China Sea. They would not be involved, except quite marginally, in a developing Chinese civil war between Chiang's nationalists and Mao Tse-tung's Communists (a different species of nationalists), which the latter would finally win by 1949.

It is significant that the Russians chose not to be involved either. The Chinese Communists got little or no help from Stalin and even less from his successors. Stalin himself had not expected that the Chinese Communists would win their civil war, until too late; he maintained normal relations with Chiang Kai-shek until almost 1949. By 1970, there was serious sporadic fighting between Russian and Chinese troops along their border rivers. By that time, the American government, led by Richard Nixon and his secretary of state, Henry Kissinger, had decided to radically improve American relations with China. A few years later Mao Tse-tung was gone, and his followers put an end to the

remaining Communist practices in the everyday life and economics of their enormous country, while keeping a Communist
Party monopoly in their domestic politics. Did this matter much
in the long run? Illusions about China, including economic and
material illusions, have been an American tendency through
more than two hundred years, in various political circumstances.
History does not repeat itself, even though historical and ideological illusions persist longer than they should.

Yet beneath and above such great developments involving the
daily lives and the destinies of billions of people across the globe,
there was an—*an,* not *the*—advance of democracy. What follows
is a necessary, though inadequate, summary.

The European Age was gone—and, together with it, one of
its precious and fragile achievements: liberal democracy. It was
(and here and there it still is) liberal democracy, often allied with
constitutional monarchy, that has established and secured the
liberties and property of an increasing number of citizens during
the past two or even three hundred years. One of its elements,
constitutional monarchy, has become less widespread in the
twentieth century, often because governments of this type were
not supported by the United States, even though the once traditional American opposition to monarchism has faded away.[3]

---

3. Consider that under a German or Austrian monarchy, Hitler would not have risen to
power; that even during the Second World War and the German occupation, most of the
constitutional monarchs of Europe opposed Hitler and the Third Reich; that the king of Italy deposed Benito Mussolini in 1943; that it was the Japanese emperor, Hirohito, who led
the Japanese peace party against the militarists and was able to convince his people of the
need to end the war. (A wise American exception to antimonarchism was made by President Harry Truman in July 1945: he dropped a requirement that the coming surrender of
Japan include the deposing of the emperor.) But after 1945, the remaining monarchs in the
East, from Egypt and Iran through Indochina and Afghanistan, were unsupported by various American governments.

Throughout the world, many people saw the United States as the prime example of the idea of Progress and of the Modern Age. Yet even during the twentieth century, there were signs that the Modern Age was passing—that the twentieth was a transitional century, from the Modern (or, more precisely, European) Age to something else. Here, we should consider Alexis de Tocqueville's great—but also commonsense—vision. Nearly two hundred years ago, he, too, knew the still-current division of the history of our ancestors into its customary categories: Antique (mostly Greek and Roman), Medieval, and Modern (mostly European and then American). But he saw further, and deeper: the age of democracy, already coming into being, meant that rule by minorities was being replaced by the rule of majorities: in sum, an evolution from Aristocratic Ages to a Democratic Age. He saw, as well, that this does not simplify but instead complicates the structure of societies, their politics, their events, and their historical reconstruction. Though it is possible to ascertain what a ruler or rulers want, what "the people" want is a step removed from reality: their political and social choices are often consequent to what other people say or do in their name. A discussion of this topic is no doubt beyond the scope of this brief history of a past century, with its welter of achievements and problems.

"Conservative" and "liberal" were nineteenth-century ideologies and adjectives; but their present employment has become increasingly imprecise, and often even senseless. In any event, the traumas and advances of the twentieth century encompass the development of technology—or rather, the mechanization of ever more activities and impressions of everyday life. This has its own dangers, actual as well as potential. One example: after 1945 it became possible for large segments of humankind to destroy themselves and their world. Yet this has not happened.

Even when the American military dropped atomic bombs on two Japanese cities in August 1945, this act—despite its horrors—helped to end the Second World War. Although during the First World War there were massacres and deportations of hundreds of thousands of people (such as Armenians in Turkey), during the Second World War the systematic murder of many more millions, among them almost five million Jewish men, women, and children, was ordered and carried out by Germans, probably the most highly educated people in Europe. When nationalism replaces older versions of patriotism (every patriot is also a bit of a nationalist, but few nationalists are truly patriots), they seek enemies among their fellow citizens. Thus, since the 1940s, many states and nations have seen the emigration of millions of people. Whether the increasing admixture of different peoples will lead to a new kind of internationalism, no one knows. Popular sovereignty—alas, often dependent on nationalist sentiment—is the professed basis of most governments now.

But this book is about the history of the twentieth century, not of the twenty-first.

— 2 —

"NOW WE HAVE ONLY
PEOPLES' WARS"

A European War—1914: A short war?—But entire nations
rushing at each other—Still a war between states—Medioc-
rity of most generals—Russia withdraws from the war—
Communism: a seventy-year episode in the more than one
thousand years of Russian history—The complicated history
of America's entry into the First World War

THE WAR THAT BEGAN IN 1914 was not the first world war. If by
"world war" we mean a war between great powers fought on
more than one continent and across the seas, there were such, on
occasion, between England, Spain, and France in the four great
centuries (the sixteenth to the nineteenth) when Europe grew
and rose throughout large portions of the world. But the British
government was, by and large, correct when it designated the
War of 1914 the "European War." Unlike the previous overseas
wars and also unlike the Second World War, the War of 1914 was
a very great war, fought, save for a few exceptions, on the continent of Europe. Its results were enormous, among them the demise of four great European empires, an unprecedented redrawing of the map of Europe, and the creation of many new states,
some of them extant even now. But along with and beneath these

transformations came the profound shock that the war dealt to European civilization—a trauma probably even greater and longer-lasting than the consequences of the Second World War.

On a sun-laden early afternoon, on June 28, 1914, a Sunday, the Austrian archduke, Franz Ferdinand, eventual successor to the emperor Franz Joseph, was gunned down together with his wife in an open automobile in Sarajevo, then an obscure provincial capital in the Austro-Hungarian Empire, by a terrorist from Serbia. There had been such terrorist acts and assassinations in Europe during the years and decades before 1914. But now the Austrian government and its military chiefs decided that this horrid deed was a sufficient opportunity for Austria to punish Serbia, a Balkan state that had already made plenty of trouble before 1914. Such a military punishment might even lead to a chastened Serbia, causing the balance of power in southeastern Europe to shift in Austria's favor. This was a fatal miscalculation. A month after the assassination, Austria declared war on Serbia, dismissing the compromises that the Serbian government offered to Vienna—and then came something new and ominous: a cloud over much of Europe and Britain. Churchill, at that time First Lord of the Admiralty, would describe it this way in his incomparable prose sixteen years later. In July 1914 the members of the British cabinet, in counsel with the king, were still deeply involved with the problem of Ireland. On July 24, "in search of an exit from the deadlock, the Cabinet toiled around the muddy byways of Fermanagh and Tyrone." And then an official brought the text of the Austrian ultimatum to the British foreign secretary, Sir Edward Grey. "The parishes of Fermanagh and Tyrone faded back into the mists and squalls of Ireland and a strange light began immediately, but with perceptible gradations, to fall and grow upon the map of Europe."

Yet even three or four days later, most people in the British government, both the cabinet and Parliament, were loath to consider that even if a European war was coming, Britain would be drawn into it. Now came a concatenation of events. The Russians thought they'd better stand with Serbia; they began to mobilize their enormous far-flung armies. The Germans thought they had no option but to do the same; they had known of France's alliance with Russia since 1894, and their entire war plan rested on that. Russia was a more formidable power than France—so France had to be attacked and defeated before Russia. To achieve this swiftly, the German armies chose to march through Belgium, whose neutrality they, and Britain, had accepted almost a century before. Now they did not. By August 4, all of the Great Powers of Europe were at war.

With nary an exception, in 1914 most people, including the statesmen and military chiefs of the Great Powers, believed and acted as if this would not be a long war. They were wrong. Wrong they were, too, with their military plans, including their assessments of their enemies. Even before the end of 1914, the Austrians found that Serbia was a very hard nut to crack. In September, the Germans learned at the Marne that they could not crush the French armies, as they had in 1870. The Russians found that even with half of the German armies deployed in the west, they could not push into Germany in the east. By Christmas 1914, the First World War (the Germans and Americans had begun to name it thus) was dragging on and on. It did not resemble the wars of the recent past. It was still a war between states, but it was now a war in which entire nations were rushing at each other. Not many people had foreseen that. One was the elder Helmuth von Moltke, victor of the Franco-Prussian War in 1870–1871, who said in the Reichstag twenty years later: "The age of cabinet wars is behind us—now we have only peoples' wars." The armed states of Europe might now begin wars "whose duration and conclusion cannot be foreseen."

In 1914, millions of peoples cheered the war on. Turkey and Bulgaria came into the war, allied with the so-called Central Powers, Germany and Austria-Hungary. In 1915, the Western Powers succeeded in bribing Italy to enter the war on their side—again, with the enthusiastic acclamation of Italian public opinion, though with very little impact on the battlefields. That year brought a stalemate of sorts, but only of sorts. Fields and towns all over Europe were now strewn with ruins, gashed by vast trenches, littered with the dead and wounded bodies of hundreds of thousands of soldiers. In 1916, more than half a million French, British, and German soldiers died at Verdun and the Somme. Romania and Portugal joined the Allies, but with few effects on the course of the war. The injection of German divisions was the crucial contribution that the Austro-Hungarians needed to win this campaign or that.

Then, in 1917, came a great change: the United States entered the European War and Russia dropped out of it. The new Bolshevik pretenders ruling Russia had to sign a humiliating peace treaty with Germany and its allies in early 1918. Now the Germans began a strenuous offensive, a last attempt to crush the French and British armies and reach Paris. But the French and British held out, and by early summer of 1918 more and more American troops were being brought to the front lines.

By October, a new German government hoped that through acceptance of some of the ideas of the American president, Woodrow Wilson, they might achieve a peace that was not catastrophic. This was not so. Germany's allies, including Austria-Hungary, were breaking apart. The German armed forces surrendered on November 11, 1918. What followed was not peace but near-chaos, lasting for almost five years.

One summary conclusion: in 1918, France, Britain, and the United States were able to defeat Germany without Russia; twenty-five years later, in the Second World War, they could not. One man, Winston Churchill, foresaw some of this as early as 1930. He hoped that the Germans would not try again. But they did.

This has been a brief summary of the history of the First World War. Yet please consider that it is not superficial. I have agonized about my choice of almost every word of it. The reason for this is my conviction that history consists of words, even more than of "facts," because "facts" are inseparable from their statements, and these amount to more than the wrapping of facts; that the use and the choice of every word is not only a stylistic but a moral decision for a historian (as it is for every human being speaking). But of course the above summary leaves a lot of things out. And many of the matters I have left out contain, explicitly or implicitly, the meanings of certain events. Of those, there are a great many kinds, on a great many levels. This is not an encyclopedic book. Within my self-imposed limitations, all I can do is try.

Consider the startling condition that in August 1914, so many intelligent statesmen and military and political experts thought and said that the impending conflict was a large "thunderstorm" (this word appears often in their statements). It had long been expected, but the war would surely be brief. Wrong they were. But how and why? There were at least two reasons, I think. The first was their historical knowledge, their memories and consideration of the wars in Europe during the preceding one hundred years. Nearly all of these had lasted for less than a year, even the Franco-Prussian War. There had been ugly little wars in the Balkans in 1912 and 1913, but they had not mattered very much. The Great Powers had not been involved. All of this had little to do with the development of communications and transport systems—railways, for example. It had much to do with another element: those wars had been conflicts between states, but also between peoples. In 1914, the primary and traditional frameworks of states were stuffed with the masses of their nations.

Twenty years later, Hitler said that the state was but a restricted framework, or *Zwangsform*—that the existence of nations preceded that of modern states, and would eventually prevail over the latter. One important indication of this was the First World War, certainly the events of 1914. The detailed and valuable researches of historians have dealt mainly with the relations of states and their governments. This is understandable. Among the mountains of books about 1914, relatively few works have concentrated, for example, on the influence of the press, on the way it enthusiastically supported the war in just about every nation—and this in a period that has been called the Golden Age of the Press, due to the overall increase in literacy during the decades before 1914. And that was but one outcome of social democratization, and also of the complete failure of Marxism, with its belief in international socialism. The character, the beliefs (and the wishes) of a German worker had little in common with those of an English or French one. Furthermore, within each nation, differences in national opinions across social classes were narrower than they had been before. Despite the existence of pacifist and international socialist groups, their opposition to war melted away in the bubbling cauldron of national sentiment

like pats of cold butter (consider but the murder of the principled French socialist Jean Jaurès, in Paris, before the declarations
of war). Finally, the very composition of the armies reflected the
growth of national uniformity. In 1914, as during the Franco-
Prussian War of 1870–1871, the German army was still composed
of commanders and units from Prussia, Saxony, Bavaria, Würt-
temberg, and so on. After the First Battle of the Marne, in September 1914, many of these distinctive units lost their meaning.
Henceforth, there was an all-German army filled with German
soldiers. Even in the multinational Austro-Hungarian army, its
highly diverse national components did not become divisive or
centrifugal until almost 1918. Nor was there any significant difference between the national sentiments of the military and
those of civilians during the war—including the very large "reserves," made up of civilians and retired officers.

The significance of much of this is apparent in retrospect, as
part and parcel of the advance of a democratic age. Yet it had almost no effect on the origins of the First World War, which was
still a war between states; likewise, it did not affect the belief of
statesmen and military leaders in 1914 that this would be a dra-
matic but short European war. Their careful calculations, including those of their military planners, turned out to be wrong. The
German Schlieffen Plan, sensible and convincing, laid down the
principle that Russia was much more powerful than France, so
that in the event of a two-front war the French armies would
need to be defeated first, and soon; France would then have to
sue for peace. In 1914 (and also thereafter), the opposite occurred. The French may scarcely have "won" the Battle of the
Marne, but the Germans certainly lost it. And an infinitely more
important outcome was a new, dreadful, often senseless struggle:
an enormous war fought between trenches, eventually involving

over a million Frenchmen, even more Germans, and nearly a million Britons, soldiers who were seldom able to break forth from their trenches and front lines.

Related to this awful kind of war were not only the shortcomings of all kinds of statesmen, but also those of many of their generals. The latter were, at best, mediocre—dependent, and for too long, on their prewar practices and doctrines and their calculations; in more than a few instances, they were not only unimaginative but inadequate. The most that can be said of Joseph Joffre, the victor at the Marne, was that he was resolute. His counterpart, Moltke—descendant of the brilliant Prussian leader whose forces prevailed in 1870—was doubt-ridden, ineffective in 1914, and eventually broken in spirit. In 1918 Ferdinand Foch, commander of the vast Allied army, did an adequate job but not much more. The British generals in France were slow in 1914 and unduly cautious in 1918. (An excellent British general was Edmund Allenby, the only soldier in the history of the British army who eventually rose from private to field marshal.) Paul von Hindenburg, Erich von Falkenhayn, and Erich Ludendorff, the top Germans, were firm and resolute, but also unimaginative in their Prussian ways—altogether unlike German generals in the Second World War. There was nothing memorable in the performances of most Austrian, Hungarian, and Italian commanders. An outstanding general in 1916 was the Russian leader Aleksei Brusilov, whom even the Bolsheviks respected and promoted after the war; but by that time, it was too late for Russia. Had they kept on fighting a little longer, they would have been one of the great victors of the First World War, dominant over most of the eastern half of Europe, with consequences not unlike what was to happen at the end of the Second World War.

So this brings us to 1917, which was not a turning point in the military history of the First World War—but *was* a turning point in the entire history of the twentieth century. The United States entered Europe, while Russia dropped out of it. A year later came the military turning point of the war: the halting of the last German offensive in France by the French and British, followed by the increasing American presence and pressure on the Germans at the Western Front. These events were decisive—whereas the Russian withdrawal from Europe was not. (Something of the opposite occurred in 1941 and even thereafter: Could the Americans and the British have conquered Germany without Russia? Probably not.) In any event, after 1917 the United States and Russia—the former for the first time since its founding—became a decisive factor in the destiny of Europe. Soon, for very different reasons, both the United States and Russia would withdraw from the European scene, although this would not much matter for a while. But in 1917 and for some time in 1918, Russia's abandonment of its war against Germany was a most serious matter. It let the Germans shift a mass of troops from the Eastern Front to the Western—though ultimately with less effect than they had hoped and the Western allies had feared.

In 1917, there were two revolutions in Russia (more exactly: mostly in its then capital, St. Petersburg). The first revolution, in late February and March, was led by liberals; among other things, the tsar had to abdicate. The second and more famous revolution occurred in October and November; the Communists (in Russian: Bolsheviks) took power in St. Petersburg after the liberals and bourgeois (a small minority) were swept away at a time of chaos. In more than one way, the October events were not much of a real revolution: Lenin and his followers took control of not much more than a few abandoned government buildings in St. Petersburg. What happened afterward was something like a civil war throughout some parts of Russia, lasting for at least three years. Thereafter, the Russian Empire, renamed the Soviet Union, was ruled by the leaders of the Communist Party.

After 1917, many people, mostly in Europe, thought that the greatest danger to themselves and their civilization was Communism. After the Second World War, more people, especially Americans, believed that the entire twentieth century was marked, indeed determined, by the enormous and historic struggle between two ideologies: Communism and Democracy (or Freedom, or Capitalism). And Communism, not just Russia, had dangerous supporters in most places of the world. After the First World War, it seemed that Communism would sweep at least Central Europe; soon after the Second World War, it seemed that China and Russia, two giant Communist empires, could rule Eurasia together. None of this happened. We ought to see that even within the Soviet Union itself, Communist "rule" (my quotation marks are not accidental) was something like a seventy-year episode in the more than one-thousand-year history of the Russian state and people. After 1989, Russia did not revert to liberal democracy; it remained, and for a long time will mostly remain, the Russia it has always been.

In 1917, the—relative—success of the Bolsheviks in St. Petersburg, and then in most of the rest of the Russian Empire, was an outcome of the unpopularity of the war and of Russia's alliance with the Western Powers, very much including their ideology. The liberal and democratic new government of Russia in 1917 was unpopular for many reasons, but one of them was its insistent alliance with Britain and France, which also called for a more energetic Russian participation in the war. (Liberal statesmen such as Pavel Milyukov had suggested that the tsar's government had not been sufficiently anti-German.) The circumstance that many of the Bolsheviks had been influenced by German thinkers—of course, by Marx—was also an element, at least for a while. But first and foremost: in order for them to prevail and survive within Russia (and during a civil war), they had to reach a settlement with Germany. So in early 1918, in Brest-Litovsk, they signed a "peace" treaty with Germany and the other Central Powers, giving up considerable portions to Germany. This agreement would not last; but the Bolsheviks believed that in the chaos following the end of the First World War, some of the peoples of Europe, foremost in Eastern and Central Europe, would go Communist by themselves.

This—except for one or two short-lived and ridiculous attempts—did not happen. After 1789, the ideas and examples of the French Revolution had spread by themselves, all around France and through Western and Southern Europe. Yet for more than twenty years after 1918, until the middle of the Second World War, the Soviet Union (along with the state of Outer Mongolia) remained the only Communist regime in the world. By 1921 an "Iron Curtain" had descended, isolating the Russias from all of Europe. A quarter of a century later, Stalin would reap the consequences of Russia's mighty triumphs against Germany in the Second World War, imposing Communist regimes in many of the states of Eastern Europe. This did not last long either. Oddly, or perhaps not so oddly, anti-Communism was (and here and there still remains) the most popular ideology in the Western world. A principal beneficiary of this was to be Adolf Hitler.

———————

But meanwhile—also during the U.S. withdrawal from Europe—American influence throughout the world was, and would remain, greater, much more widespread, and at times even deeper than Russia's influence, whether Communist or not. Under the rule of Stalin, Russia turned from internationalism to a nationalist Communism (also in other superficially "Communist" statelets around the world). That, too, was short-lived.

The entry of the United States into the First World War is a simple—but also a complicated—matter. Simple, in the sense that the presence of American troops in Europe decided the war in favor of the Western Powers. Complicated, because of the historical question: How did this come about? In 1914, it never occurred to the vast majority of Americans that the United States would (or, even more, should) get involved in this new war in Europe. Less than three years later, in 1917, the majority of the American people cheered their war declaration against Germany and the entry of American armies and navies into Europe for the first time in the history of the American republic.

This was—and still is—perhaps a classic, if not *the* classic, example for historians willing to ponder that the study and reconstruction of history in the democratic age is, and will be, almost infinitely more complicated than the history, including the international history, of earlier ages (and this in spite of the shortsighted belief that the availability of documents is one of the benefits of democracy). It involves, too, the important but always questionable and necessarily imprecise study of "public opinion," which is often hardly separable from what we might call "popular sentiment." The two are not the same, but they overlap. "Public-opinion research" (including its unavoidable imprecisions) was not widespread in the United States at the time of the First World War; but here and there, public opinion was still distinguishable from popular sentiment. The former was largely an attribute of educated people, socially recognizable figures, contributors to and readers of newspapers, members of the middle and upper classes. (This very list ought to suggest the ambiguities and difficulties involved in defining groups within the ever moiling and moving formless panorama of American society.)

Many excellent books have been written about the American move toward war in the years 1914 to 1917. Most of them are valuable because of their precise description of successive events. Some of their authors have been aware of many influences, including those of the press, the latter having been a formative source of public opinion. Important, too, is that the upper strata of American society (there were of course exceptions) were largely Anglophiles, while American populists were not. Also important were the great events in the Atlantic (including the ways in which they were reported and represented)—for example, the Germans' sinking of the *Lusitania* in April 1915 (a British ship, but it carried hundreds of Americans to their deaths), and the temporary German suspension of unconditional submarine warfare in 1916, resumed in January 1917. Altogether, British and pro-British propaganda in the United States was much more effective than the often clumsy German propaganda efforts. Yet the ranking of evidence and of factors that led to the American declaration of war against Germany in April 1917 is necessarily inadequate. For the sentiments (and also some of the opinions) of the American people were not simple. Most Americans believed in the superiority of the New World to the Old. Many of them also believed that it was the proper thing, if not America's duty, to send an army "over there" and teach the Old World a lesson. Again, many of them believed that this was also, and perhaps even foremost, a war of Democracy against German Imperialism. (The abdication of the tsar in Russia in early 1917 seemed to have eliminated the unpleasant situation in which the United States was allied to an imperial monarchy.) And so it seemed—at least for a while. For once, there are numbers to support the use of the words "many" and "most." The U.S. Congress approved the declaration of war by a vote of 393 to 50—a ratio that seems to reflect, not inaccurately, the division of the American people at the time.

All of these complexities existed, too, in the mind and spirit of the president, Woodrow Wilson. He had been elected president in 1912 because the Republican Party was divided: their majority did not want to grant Theodore Roosevelt a third term. This was lamentable, perhaps even tragic, a fact of which many Americans are still unaware. With all of his faults, Theodore Roosevelt was a great man. His knowledge of the world, of other nations, and even of history was far wider and better than that of the one-time college professor Woodrow Wilson. Had Roosevelt been the American president in 1914, the entire history of the First World War would have been different, and perhaps shorter.

But this is not the place for such speculations. It is sufficient to state that the American entry into the war in 1917 had long-range as well as short-range consequences. In the democratic age, especially, it is more difficult to conclude a war than to begin one. Many of the great mistakes of the peacemaking in 1918 and after were due to Wilson. More important and more enduring was the ideology he bequeathed to the American people—an ideology of global universalism ("What is good for America is good for the world") whose occasional benefits were not comparable to its many and enduring shortcomings. (Subsequent American leaders, Republicans as well as Democrats, who were to a considerable extent admirers of Wilson include Herbert Hoover, Franklin Roosevelt, John Foster Dulles, Richard Nixon, Bill Clinton, and George W. Bush.) In this respect, too, the ideas and choices of this pale professor president outlasted those of his contemporary Lenin, with consequences evident even now. Such is the irony of history—and such are the complexities of human minds.

"NATIONAL SELF-DETERMINATION"

A "new Europe"? Yes and no—The end of four great empires? Yes and no—Peace treaties and their grave faults—
Consequences in Asia—"Central Europe" the crux, again

"UNCONDITIONAL SURRENDER" IS AN imprecise phrase or
principle, since there are implicit (sometimes even explicit) compromises included in every surrender. If the principle is accepted
by both sides, unconditional surrender ends a war at once. This
was not always so after the First World War, in 1918. The war
ended with armistices here and there, chaotically and gradually
elsewhere. A kind of settling down did not occur until 1923—
that, too, with a sense of incompleteness, especially among the
loser states. During the war there had been some talk about a
"New Europe," an idea or ideal supported by a few liberal thinkers and international "experts" in England; it had few effects and
echoes. An entirely fresh, imaginative, and radical proposal for a
new Europe (called Pan-Europe) appeared in 1923, drafted by a
cosmopolitan Austrian nobleman; it had many echoes but no
real effects. I may return to this by and large estimable effort a
little later—but even at this point it may be worth noticing that it
came from Austria, where, as also in Germany after 1930, quite
another new and dynamic political force began to rise, eventu-

ally leading to a second world war eight or nine years later. Its unexpected and unusual leader was an Austrian, Adolf Hitler, who united Germany and then Austria and who alone among all other statesmen in the world chose to begin a second world war in 1939, which he and his German-speaking people almost won.

In Hitler's life and mind, too, the end of the First World War was a sudden, shocking turning point. He had been a volunteer in that war (in the German not the Austrian army); he found himself—"found himself" may be *the* mot juste—in a military hospital in November 1918. He would later describe this awakening in his famous autobiography, *Mein Kampf,* and there is no reason to question the importance of his "finding himself." There had not been anything very unusual in his thoughts during his youth and in his respectable military service during the war. In 1918 he entered the thirtieth year of his life. His chosen fatherland (Germany) and his actual motherland (Austria) had been defeated. Sparked by these shattering events, his views of the world crystallized. He suddenly knew great tragedy, comparable to his loss of his beloved mother years before—the persistent grief of a deeply attached son. Then and there (he wrote), "I decided to become a politician." One result of his decision was nothing less than a second world war.

No one could have imagined anything like this in 1918 or for long years after. The end of the First World War brought a sense of relief to the victor nations, though little else. One popular reaction in November 1918 occurred in London, where the news of the Armistice brought a day and night of wild public revels unprecedented in British history. There were few such popular outbursts elsewhere, except perhaps in some of the newly founded states; the map of Europe was redrawn more drastically at the war's end than perhaps at any time before or after, because of the victory of the Western Allies and because of the partial dissolution of great European empires that had existed for centuries. This was the most important change. The German Empire was diminished; its monarchy was eliminated. Yet less than twenty years later, a new Germany became the greatest power in Europe. Not only did the Austro-Hungarian monarchy cease to exist, but that old traditional state and empire was splintered into half a dozen component states; further portions were given to other countries, which acquired new frontiers, many of which exist even now. The Russian Empire, as we have seen, had already extinguished its monarchy in 1917; and the price for the survival of its new and weird Bolshevik regime was the reduction of the old Russian state, with four or five new states and nations coming into being along its former western edge. (They, too, largely ceased to exist by 1940, though they reappeared another fifty years later.) One minor exception to the disappearance of monarchies was Bulgaria, an ally of the Central Powers; its kingdom continued to exist until the end of another world war, in 1946. The great exception was Turkey, whose Ottoman Empire fell apart in 1918, after which it became something like a military dictatorship under the rule of a formidable general, Mustafa Kemal. He struck down and replaced traditional Turkish customs and institutions with strokes of his imperious fist, but also accepted the ending of the former and now-fragile Ottoman rule over a number of nations and statelets in the Near East (Egypt, Syria, Palestine, Lebanon, Iraq, and so on)—an amputation that did Turkey little harm but much good.

In 1919 and 1920, much of this was arranged through the peace treaties with Germany, Austria, Hungary, Bulgaria, and Turkey, drawn up and then signed in Versailles and other suburbs of Paris by the Western and associated powers. Even though President Wilson, during an absence from Washington unprecedented for an American president, was in Paris for many weeks in the spring of 1919, the United States chose not to be either a signatory or a guarantor of these treaties. Peacemaking in 1919 was a sorry succession of events, many of them due to the shortcomings of the peacemakers themselves. On the map of Europe, eight new states came into existence—a diminished and truncated Austria, Poland, Finland, Estonia, Latvia, Lithuania, Czechoslovakia, and Hungary (not independent before 1919)—plus a conglomeration of three Slavic nations: Serbia, Croatia, and Slovenia, called SHS, later transmogrified into something named Yugoslavia. Twenty years after 1919, many of these entities had ceased to exist, often because they had been broken up; the only unbroken and surviving state was Finland (which, too, had to give up some of its territory to the Soviet Union in 1940). Most of them adopted parliamentary forms of government; yet within ten years after 1919, they would abandon their liberal and bourgeois structures, due to many circumstances, including the thinness and weakness of their middle classes.

Meanwhile, however weakened in the short term, a united Germany and a united Russia remained in existence. One reason for this was the shortsightedness of the peacemaking powers. Another was the inclination to vengeance and the insistence on security by the temporary victors. Yet another reason was the insufficient attention that was devoted, perhaps especially by the British (despite a large group of experts accompanying them), to some of these treaties; the petty work preoccupied their envoys and diplomatists for more than a year, and some of the details were neglected. All of these treaties were discussed and signed—with little or no participation allowed to their victims—in Versailles, St. Germain, Neuilly, Trianon, and Sèvres, with Germany,

Austria, Bulgaria, Hungary, and Turkey, respectively. No peace treaty is ever cheered by the defeated; but in 1919 and 1920, an unusual amount of humiliation was imposed on the temporarily powerless victims. The armaments and the size of a now-remnant German army were drastically reduced; those of the German navy even more so; along the Rhine an Allied occupation force was stationed, ostensibly to guarantee Germany's payment of its penalties, exaggerated sums as these were; Germany was obliged to accept prime responsibility for the war in 1914; Germany and Austria were forbidden to attempt any kind of union; pieces of imperial Germany, especially Alsace-Lorraine and a portion of mostly German-inhabited lands, were given to France and Poland. This is an incomplete list; but what was probably the most injurious was the transfer of large German, Austrian, Hungarian, and Bulgarian populations to other states and sovereignties. The most extreme redrawing of states and of their frontiers affected Hungary, which lost two-thirds of its former lands, including more than three million Hungarians, to Czech, Slovak, Romanian, Serbian, Croatian, and even Austrian and Italian rule.

Much of this was done despite the principle declared and espoused by President Wilson as late as 1918, about the primary values and merits of "national self-determination." Little of that had been considered seriously by the Western Allies before. But by 1918, they were exhausted enough to accept it, often thoughtlessly and impractically. All of this was happening at the very time when Wilson and his administration had largely abandoned their support for these principles—indeed, when the United States had chosen to withdraw from Europe, evacuating its troops. Hence, the United States was neither a signatory nor the guarantor of some of these treaties. The League of Nations—

another favorite cause and brainchild of Wilson—was then set up in Geneva. The attractiveness of such a new institution in international affairs evoked much liberal support both in Europe and America, but that, too, was short-lived. The French prime minister, Georges Clemenceau, hoped for a lasting, even permanent Anglo-American-French alliance guaranteeing the frontiers and the security of France—but this did not come about. He also thought that most of these new successor states in Eastern Europe should be allies of France—another military and political guarantee for France in the unspeakable case of another German-French war. That, too, did not last. Less than twenty years after 1919, the once-impressive alliance system of France with Czechoslovakia, Yugoslavia, Romania, and even Poland had become worthless.

Many of the new Communist rulers of Russia were internationalists. They believed and planned that Communism in Russia would repeat itself in other countries, especially in Eastern and Central Europe, including Germany. This did not happen. There had been—perhaps—more reason to think that peoples and nations, and their Communists, closest to Russia would follow the Russian "example." That did not happen either. One reason for this was that most of these people rejected Russian rule, whether they were Communist or not. During the Russian civil war, they (unlike the British and French governments, at least for a while) did not support the anti-Bolshevik armies and their generals, knowing that the latter wanted to reestablish the old Russian Empire. Nor did they have any illusions about the Bolsheviks, whether they were Russians or not. They fended them off with arms. Lenin and his cohorts thought this was a temporary situation, which it was not. By 1920, the "White" (that is, anti-Communist) armies, and their support by the Western Allies, were fading away. Now Lenin and his people chose to think that the main instrument of the advance of Communism into Central Europe would be military power, the Red Army. They had reasons to fight the new Poland, whose army in early 1920 penetrated well into the Ukraine. The result was the Russian-Polish war of 1920, with its unexpected consequences. The Red Army now pushed the Poles back and advanced to the outskirts of Warsaw. There, in August 1920, the Poles defeated the Russians, who had to retreat several hundred miles to the east, into Belorussia and the western Ukraine. Now Lenin and his followers realized that in order to maintain their power within Russia itself, they needed peace—or, rather, no more wars with their enemies. So in 1920 and 1921, they signed a series of treaties with their western neighbors, including Poland and Finland, along frontiers that were mainly favorable to the latter two countries. That also meant a diminution and the enforced isolation of the new Soviet Union itself. Thereafter the Soviet Union was recognized, diplomatically, as yet another—though unpleasant—state by all of the other states of the world (except for the United States, Hungary, Switzerland, and Yugoslavia, but eventually that would come about, too).

Sooner rather than later, the Russian Bolsheviks learned that national allegiances, traditions, opinions, and sentiments were more powerful than ideologies, especially international ones. Also that "powerful" meant something more than popular; it had to be demonstrated by determined men—even at the risk of international condemnation. The sterling examples of this were Turkey and Greece. The former was, rather thoughtlessly, punished by Britain and France (and Italy, too), who reduced the Ottoman Empire to a badly truncated statelet through the Treaty of Sèvres in 1920, which robbed Turkey of large traditional provinces inhabited by many Greeks. Despite Turkey's late and not very decisive joining with the Central Powers during the First World War, it did not deserve such treatment. Its new leader, Kemal, saw that four years after the First World War, France and Britain were not willing to fight another war in the Near East. So in 1922 he and his Turkish soldiers fought a small war with Greece, expelling masses of Greek people from Asia Minor, where the latter had been denizens for hundreds of years. A new treaty, signed in Lausanne in 1923 by Turkey and Greece and governed by the Western Powers, redrew the frontiers and began a new chapter of relations between these two ancient enemies. It also showed to the world, especially to Europeans, that the Paris peace treaties could be overturned by force sooner or later.

This book is a (short) history of the twentieth century; and my readers, especially now, may question why much of it until now has dealt with the history of Europe, rather than with that of the rest of the world. This emphasis will change as we go along, but there is at least one primary reason for this almost unilateral perspective from 1914 to 1923. We have seen that the First World War was primarily, and almost entirely, a European war (though there were marginal combats between some European Powers in Africa and in the Near East). We have also seen that the decisive outcome of this greatest of wars involved the United States and Russia; but then, for very different reasons, the Russian and American empires both withdrew from Europe after the end of the war.

Despite these political and strategic withdrawals, the influence of America grew in the lives and thoughts of many European people, while those of Russia did not. Thus, from about 1919 to 1939, it seemed not only that America's influence existed even while its "isolation" from Europe had been declared, but the primacy of Europe within the great panorama of world history prevailed again. In 1939, the Second World War started as a European war (which was what Hitler wanted it to be), but it did not remain one. The colonial possessions of the French, British, Spanish, Belgian, and Portuguese empires had remained largely unchanged. Some of them now included pre-1914 German colonies; some of them reformed the conditions of their colonial administrations, but these did not come to an end until the Second World War. There were signs of native nationalism and anticolonialism, but with few effects—except, and this *was* a considerable effect—that by the 1920s there were signs that the minds of the Western European peoples and of their intellectuals were no longer deeply attached to their colonial empires. For a few years after 1919, the Communist Russian rulers and their worldwide supporters believed that the victory of an anti-imperialist, anticolonialist, and antiracist new Russia would result in new governments and leaders in Turkey or Persia or Afghanistan, new natural allies of the Soviet Union. That, too, did not happen. With very few exceptions, the new nationalist and anticolonial dictators—whether a Kemal in Turkey, or a Reza Shah in Persia, or an Amanullah in Afghanistan, or later Chiang Kai-shek in China—chose to have little to do with Russia and nothing at all to do with their own native Communists, whom they killed off as soon as they could.

One great (and, throughout the two world wars, durable) exception was Japan. It had begun its modernization decades before 1914; it had proceeded to establish its military and political primacy in Korea and in some of China before 1914; it had defeated Russia in a splendid little war in 1905, with a very modern navy. Indeed, during the First World War, the British (more than the Americans) welcomed the presence of Japanese warships in many seas. So Japan was one of the victors of the First World War, expanding in many places to an extent that caused anxiety in Washington and even among the American people. It was natural and expectable that after the war there should be some kind of disarmament, including a reduction in the enormous American, British, and Japanese war fleets left over from the First World War. Therefore a conference assembled in Washington in 1921–1922. It was a notable achievement of the administration of Warren Harding, otherwise a president largely indifferent to foreign affairs. The main architect of this conference was Charles Evans Hughes, Harding's estimable and excellent secretary of state. The participant powers agreed to a 5:5:5:3:3 ratio of battleship tonnages, including Japan, which largely kept to the agreement until 1934, when it chose to be no longer bound by any such naval restrictions. Another instrument, the so-called Nine-Power Treaty restricting all of the foreign powers from expanding further in China, was a positive agreement that did not last long either. Meanwhile, the British-Japanese Treaty of 1902, amounting to a near-alliance, expired in 1922 and was not renewed. It was a sign of Britain's primary preference for good relations with the United States over those with Japan.

But in Europe (and also in Asia Minor) it took another year until the revolutionary or other chaotic conditions settled down. This was so especially in Germany, where moiling and roiling sentiments broke out in sporadic and sometimes violent revolutions, from November 1918 until they petered out as late as 1923. After that, grave political crises were relatively rare for about eight or nine years. This was the only semblance of peace between the two world wars, separating somehow the immediate consequences of the First World War from the preludes of the Second, which began to appear soon after Hitler's assumption of power in Germany in 1933.

———————

This is at least one reason why, in this short history of the twentieth century, I am compelled to devote a page or two to the histories of Germany and Austria after the First World War, including the consequences of their military defeat in 1918. The Germans, by and large, are not an excitable people, not revolutionary in temperament, not likely to accept disorder. But the phrase "by and large," while explaining much, is also an imperfect generalization. The shock of 1918, for the Germans, cut deep and lasted long. The French revolutionary examples and ideas in and after 1789 had had German followers, but not everywhere and not much. Same with the bourgeois revolutionary wave that swept Europe in 1848. But in 1918 and after, many Germans were affected by a sense of "Götterdämmerung," a sometimes Wagnerian emotion about the end of an entire world. Oswald Spengler's influential book *Der Untergang des Abendlandes* (literally, *The Sinking of the West*), a large book, was published a few months before the military defeat in 1918. It had a significant echo in the minds and hearts of many Germans, spreading beyond Germany too. The respect for France, and indeed for the ideology of the Enlightenment, was gone. Spengler not only dismissed but denied the worth of most bourgeois achievements. The mutinies and working-class revolts of November 1918 did not last, though some of them were repeated during the next five years, including a short-lived and sometimes ludicrous Soviet-style republic in Munich, swept away by a hostile Bavarian population together with the German army.

The popular respect for the latter (however reduced in size and armaments by the Versailles Treaty) remained high after the First World War and throughout the Second. The army easily crushed revolutionary insurgencies, including one by the extreme nationalist Right in 1920 and another in November 1923 in Munich, where, for the first time, Hitler played a considerable role. Before and after that, the political and popular attraction and influence of the Left, including not only Communists but the respectable and moderate German Social Democratic Party, declined. For a long time, more Germans read (or attempted to read) *The Sinking of the West* than *Mein Kampf,* even after the purchase and the reading of the latter became near-compulsory. Bourgeois institutions and the bourgeois temperament, especially when associated with the victors of Britain and France, had little impact in the now democratized and constitutionalized Weimar Republic in Germany, where something new was beginning and growing. This was the ideology—rather than the "philosophy"—of National Socialism. International socialism, the economic and materialist principle declared by Karl Marx and others—that classes meant more than states everywhere, but particularly in Europe—was superficially logical but profoundly wrong. Among many instances of his shortsightedness, Marx overlooked the existence of nations; he failed to see that nations and states were not the same things, and that national sentiments, perhaps especially in an age of mass politics, were often more powerful than state interests. This was (or should have been) already evident in 1914 and even more afterward. Consciousness of national identity was much more important than class-consciousness. This was true in almost every nation and class, in one way or another.

Such awareness of nationalism was more anticapitalist than

antisocialist—capitalism being sometimes, though not predominantly. international. Early in the twentieth century, a few small political parties chose to declare and name themselves "national socialists." (One example: Czech national socialists in Bohemia, sharply separating themselves from their German counterparts.) After 1920, the presence and the influence of nationalist socialism spread, especially in Central Europe. Their emphasis on the adjective "nationalist" was obvious. In Germany, this was almost immediately recognized by their opponents, who hoped to ridicule them by using the abbreviation "Nazi-Sozi," for "Nationalist-Sozialist." Now, note that from this abbreviation the "Sozi" very soon disappeared, while the "Nazi" remained, showing that it was much more important than the "Sozi" half of the adjective.

Hitler understood this. Even though he got the support of other German nationalists who were not socialists, he eventually won the support of masses of former socialists too. Here the example of Austria is telling. The Austrian Social Democratic Party, like its German counterpart, was substantial and fairly respectable; after the war, it had the support of most Austrian voters. But Austrians, like Germans, thought and felt that they had been wrongly punished by the peace treaties, which shifted a few million German-speaking Austrians to Czechoslovakia, Yugoslavia, Italy. As a result, most Austrians in 1920 were for a German Austria, meaning some kind of union with Germany on the basis of national self-determination. The Allies prohibited this (among other things, it would have made Germany larger than it had been before 1914), as late as 1931, when France opposed a German-Austrian customs union. More significantly, in Austria, too, a local National Socialist Party began to attract adherents when the two other large parties weakened. It also profited from the presence of Austrian anti-Semites, especially among univer-

sity students. Very telling was the quite illogical designation of
an Austrian "nationalist": an Austrian-born person who preferred to disregard his "Austrian" identity, as well as his loyalty to
the Austrian state. He was a German-Austrian, or plainly a German, and partisan of an Austrian union with Germany. All of
this worked to the advantage of Hitler, even before 1933. By that
time, the Austrian Nazis were threatening to become a large
party within Austria too.

After the French revolutionary and Napoleonic wars, there
came a conservative reaction in much of Europe. It did not last
long, though it was a reaction espoused not only by the restored
monarchies, but in some ways by many of the peoples themselves. After the First World War, there was no such reaction—
no popular or intellectual longing for anything like Victorian-
ism. There was a subdued overcast grayness over much of Europe
and in the minds of many Europeans. Optimism about the future was far from prevalent. Meanwhile, America was a place of
bright lights and untold riches. By 1918 the American dollar had
replaced the British pound as the primary and most stable currency in the world. Still, the United States was far away.

Much of this widespread pessimism and insecurity was apparent in the loss of the value of money. Inflation, not deflation,
afflicted most European states after 1918. The Money Age was
the nineteenth century, not the twentieth—not only because of
the near-universal gold standard, but because of the confidence
in the national currencies. (In France, for example, throughout
most of the nineteenth century, including wars and three revolutions, the value of the French franc remained largely stable.) For
a while, the postwar governments did little to control inflation.
The classic case was Germany, where by 1923 the gradual inflation after 1918 had accelerated to fantastic proportions—some-

thing that the German people remembered and avoided after their much greater catastrophe in the Second World War and also generations later, even to the present day. Then, near the end of 1923 or soon afterward, the governments of Europe introduced new currencies, which were accepted with a measure of relief. Once again, something like an exhausted peace spread over much of Europe, without anything like nostalgia for or a wish to return to the past—to the world before 1914.

— 4 —

"COSSACKS! BRETHREN!"

Communists—The nature of their fears—The situation of
the Jews

IN THE HISTORY OF THE world, the Communist revolution in
Russia in 1917 was an anomaly. Seventy years after Marx's *Communist Manifesto,* the majority of the working classes everywhere
were mostly indifferent to Communism. There were no successful Communist revolutions anywhere except in Russia—a country that Marx (at least for a long time) categorically excluded
from his projections of Communism. All this is well known. Less
well known is the evidence of how afraid the Communist leaders
were of their nationalist opponents. A few days before (and also
during) their uprising in St. Petersburg, Lenin's cohorts thought
it useful to address the Cossack regiments in St. Petersburg on
posters with the heading: "Cossacks! Brethren!"—this to the
most feared and hated military units of the tsarist regime. The
Bolsheviks were right: the Cossacks in 1917 were not inclined to
risk their skins in defense of Kerensky and Co., those loquacious
townies in their frock coats. Further evidence is protean. In the
Communists' short-lived attempts in Europe in 1919 (in cities
such as Munich and Budapest)—including their repulsive acts of
terrorism—there was always an underlying and often very ap-

parent fear: fear of their unpopularity, fear of their enemies, not only among the former ruling classes but also among the masses.

Of course a sense of fear, like all other primal human phenomena, is not simple and is often allied and combined with hatred. But it is an acceptable generalization to state that, at least in the Western world, the ideas of Communist and pro-Communist intellectuals in the twentieth century were inseparable from their fears: their fears of oppressive Capitalism and its agents; fear of "fascists," of "reactionaries," of nationalist crowds, of the conspiratorial powers of their opponents—a fear compensated or, rather, clothed by their intellectual belief that their ideology was the only progressive one, marking their path to the future, their future.

This does not mean that all Communists were cowards. A sense of fear and an inclination to cowardice are not always the same thing. Courage is the ability to overcome fear; this is something that every combat soldier knows in the marrow of his bones. But asseverations of psychoanalysis do not belong in this short history of the twentieth century; as Samuel Johnson wisely said, "Intentions must be gathered from acts." Telling for our purposes is the history of the Soviet Union after Lenin's death in 1924: there were substantial changes, enacted and instituted by Joseph Stalin, who was not well known before that but became the master of that vast country for the next twenty-eight years, encompassing, among other things, the Second World War.

Stalin recognized two matters, of which the second may have been even more important—and decisive—than the first, even though the first led to mass misery and famine and the death of probably more than one million people. This was collectivized agriculture: two Latinate words that do not convey their enormous impact—namely, the forcing of many millions of peasants to move from their dwellings and land to very large state-ordered and supervised farms, food-production factories. In this way, Stalin aimed to increase Russian agricultural production. The eventual results of this most radical plan were dubious; yet because of the habitual passivity of the Russian peasantry, there were few grave political effects. Before 1930, little had changed in the everyday life of the people who lived and worked in the Russian countryside, but it would no longer remain thus.

One of the aims of Stalinite policy was to put an end to many practices and tendencies in the Soviet Union that had accompanied the Bolshevik takeover in and after 1917. The elimination and prohibition of such radical and seemingly avant-garde cultural activities began in 1926. It was part and parcel of something much more important in the long run. This was the promotion of Russian nationalism at the expense of Communist internationalism (which, after all, was one of the main attractions of Communist intellectuals scattered throughout the world). Stalin was not an internationalist. He had advanced upward in the Moscow hierarchy because of his direct and often brutal ability to get rid of his actual or potential opponents within the party when needed. In 1924, he was elected party leader, the successor to Lenin, who had died that January. Within two years he was able to eliminate his main enemy, Leon Trotsky, forcing him to leave the Soviet Union. The Stalin-Trotsky duel was, and remains, telling. Trotsky was an international Communist and something of an intellectual; Stalin was not. They were natural opponents, enemies not only in their ideologies but in their very personalities, in their very backgrounds. (Fourteen years later, Stalin sent an agent to murder Trotsky, then forlorn and powerless, living somewhere in Mexico.)

More important and significant than this was the development of Stalin's thinking, of which we have only a few, scattered, but telling indications in the decade before 1939, when he would not only welcome but agree to a world-shattering pact with Hitler a few days before the outbreak of the Second World War. Stalin was a secretive man, but here and there he made remarks to the effect that internationalism was impractical, if not outdated, and that he and we must now consider nationalism seriously. "We," because this corresponded with the very transformation of the Soviet Union's leadership. A considerable number of leading commissars in Lenin's early government were Jews—in a country where Judeophobia was widespread and at times deep. By 1938, there were few Jews among the top leadership of the Soviet Communist Party. The exceptions were some officials in the foreign service (including the commissar for foreign affairs, Maxim Litvinov), whom Stalin kept, presumably because of their international knowledge and connections. Other exceptions, though of minuscule importance, were some exiled foreign Communists put into a house or two in Moscow—a sop to the idea of international Communism but devoid of any influence on Stalin.

Now this brings me to a sensitive and difficult topic that I think I cannot and should not exclude even from a short history of the twentieth century—namely, the history of the (mostly European) Jews in this period. We know that more than five million Jews were killed, or lost their lives, during the Second World War. The Holocaust was not a footnote to the Second World War, as at least one French anti-Semite (Jean-Marie Le Pen) recently declared. It belonged to the center of that conflict, because it was a principal element in the public and possibly also in the private decisions and statements of Adolf Hitler, the architect of the war. But even if Hitler had not existed, the presence (and to many people, the problem) of Jews and their influence in many countries would belong to the history of the twentieth century.

Entire libraries, including scholarly works, have been devoted to the history of the Jews; but there, too, the twentieth century is more than a new chapter, and not only because of the enormity of the Holocaust. To analyze or describe or even sum up the thousands of years of the Jewish people and of their trials does not belong in this book, except to state that the arguments for their past segregations, discriminations, occasional persecutions, and so on, for at least two thousand years, were religious, though often inseparable from racial or national sentiments. But, again, mostly around 1870, there was a change. It was then that the term "anti-Semitism" appeared, a word and adjective still current now, in spite of its fundamental inaccuracy (Jews are not necessarily Semites, nor are all Semitic peoples relatives of Jews or of Judaism). The term immediately connotes something not religious but racial. Moreover, it includes people who are no longer Jewish by religion but have converted to other, mostly Christian churches, suggesting, among other things, that they are still Jewish in their sentiments and beliefs, and consequently are dangerous elements within the nations they inhabit. This was a popular and powerful tendency in Spain during the sixteenth century— but even then, the Inquisition was concerned with the authenticity of the religious beliefs of the *conversos,* not with their nationality.

Around the nineteenth century, two new developments occurred, which gave rise to the new "anti-Semitism." The first was the very great increase in Jewish populations in many countries of Europe and in parts of the United States. In 1800, perhaps as many as 80 or 90 percent of Jews in the world lived within the confines of the Russian Empire and Poland, where they were often subject not only to restrictions but also occasionally to murderous hostility. By 1900, their mass migration westward was slowing to a trickle, while in countries such as Hungary, Romania, and Austria the Jewish population had grown from 1 to 5 percent, or even more, in a century. Much larger was their presence in some of the West's capital cities: in Vienna, Jews accounted for 14 percent of the population; in Budapest, 21 percent; in New York, almost 30 percent; in Paris, more than 5 percent. Much of this increase was due to the characteristics of that entire century, with its governing ideas of progress and liberalism and with its emphasis on industry and commerce. A consequence of this was the lifting of the remaining legal restrictions of Jews by various European governments (except for Russia and Romania). But a deeper and more populist consequence was a new kind of hostility to Jews.

By the early twentieth century, there were politicians, public figures, and writers who believed that their principal task was to alert their countrymen to the extent of the presence and sinister influence of Jews within their nations—especially in fields such as finance, banking, journalism, and other professions open to them. There were even small political parties whose leaders believed and claimed that this Jewish "problem" was the principal problem of their nation. They represented something like a new extreme Right. Before 1914—indeed, 1918—they had been read and listened to, but they had not gotten very far. One reason for this was that the mass migration from the Russias westward was diminishing. Another reason was that the reception of thousands of Jews by their host nations did not mean that they were enthusiastically embraced. Beyond their emancipation, Jews continued to be subject to political, legal, and social restrictions, limited though these were. With few exceptions, they were excluded from the high commands of armies, from high diplomatic posts, from the presidencies of important institutions, and from the leadership of political parties; they were unwelcome in certain neighborhoods and schools; and so forth. Much of this was true even in the United States. It no doubt caused great frustration and hurt, but did not inflict very much harm. (One exception was the Catholic Church. Though its members and spokesmen were often strongly anti-Semitic after 1870, the Vatican welcomed converts, elevating some of them to important bishoprics.)

The main threat to the Jews was the new nationalism, growing in popularity often among the young, especially in certain countries such as Germany and Austria. Jews were regarded as an alien people; it was believed that there was and should be no place for them—including current and former converts—within a national community. Thus, we may see, especially in Europe, another element in this new Judeophobia integral to the rise of nationalisms after 1870, and then principally after 1918. Before that, Jews had often been disliked by other people not only because of their seemingly outlandish religion but also because of their outlandish habits: strange clothing, strange beards, strange speech, and so on—a visible minority. But now, the especial hatred toward and concern with Jews was, almost everywhere, directed against assimilated Jews, who, outwardly, were often hardly distinguishable from the non-Jewish people around them. The antagonism was racial and also spiritual. To many people,

Jews represented—indeed, they incarnated—a perceived peril, perhaps a peril to the entire nation.

In many places and for many people, this was aggravated after 1918 by the presence of many Jews among the new Bolshevik rulers of Russia. "Jewish Bolshevism" became a current phrase for at least two decades. We shall see that for Hitler, Jews and Communists were the principal enemies; in 1918, he believed they were instrumental to his nation's defeat. Thereafter, he would often use the term "Jewish Bolshevism." But a careful examination of his public statements and private expressions may suggest that he did not really believe the two terms were equivalent. He hated Jews more than he hated Communists; but he also knew that the pairing of the two, along with the equivalence attributed to them, was useful, because it could be quite popular. So he kept up this popular usage, especially after 1941—so much so, that he used the phrase "Jewish Bolshevism" during his last public speech, in April 1945, shortly before his death. Yet there are ample instances of his admiration for Stalin, and for his recognition that the latter's Soviet Union was not at all Jewish-ruled.

One of the fundamental remaining differences between extremes of the Right and those of the Left is that hatred moves the former; fear, the latter. It was not always thus. Two hundred years ago, the old Right—authoritarian kingdoms and dukedoms, the conservatives and the aristocracies and the police—were fearful of the ideas of the French Revolution, of their attractions and their potential representatives. The Left (comprising young people then, but not now) hated such regimes, their rulers, and the police; when they feared them, that fear was mixed with contempt.

Then, around 1870, came a change. Nationalism was replacing the older forms of patriotism, and it proved to be an even stronger and more lasting cement binding masses of people than their sentiments about class struggle. Its extreme representations and incarnations involved even more than a dislike of foreigners. It included a contemptuous hatred of men and women within their own country whom such nationalists saw as being largely, even treasonably, non-nationalistic. This was not an aristocratic or conservative phenomenon, but a populist one. It manifested itself in a great variety of nations and states; it attracted many revolutionary young people; and their opponents, especially Jews, soon learned to fear them.

Hatred is stronger than fear. Both exist among animals. But in the human world, hatred eventually becomes self-destructive; it does not always prevail in the long run, while fear often does. Still, this can be no consolation to those who either experience or comprehend the power of hatred over fear in the short run. Besides, hatred, even more than fear, may also involve participation: people hate what they hate in themselves, or they often hate who or what is close to them. What is vengeance but the wish to cause suffering in order to heal one's own suffering? "In the spirit of revolt," Georges Bernanos wrote, "there is a principle of hatred or contempt for mankind. I'm afraid that the rebel will never be capable of bearing as much love for those he loves as he bears hatred for those he hates."

Toward the ends of the political-ideological spectrum, we may, then, observe the presence of fear among people of the radical Left and the presence of hatred among people of the radical Right. But such phenomena are not restricted to extremist believers. There exist fellow travelers on the Left but also on the Right; the latter are people whose fears are transmuted by the pleasant feeling that they are being admitted to the company of nationalists. These are not categories but tendencies. Nor are these inclinations simply attributable to the attractions of political ideologies. They are human characteristics and therefore complex ones—inclinations and potentialities that are neither fixed nor determined. They are not explainable by such definitions as "the Authoritarian Personality" or "the Totalitarian Temptation."

Men and women do not *have* ideas. They *choose* them.

5

NO NOSTALGIA FOR THE "WORLD OF YESTERDAY"

Uniqueness of the United States—Its influence different from that of other great powers—Its prosperity in the 1920s —The 1920s: the first (and perhaps the only) "modern" decade—"Depression" in and after 1929, but also American optimism: not much fear and not much hatred

THE HISTORY OF THE United States differs from that of other great empires. It would be imprecise and also exaggerated to call the eighteenth century the "French century" or the nineteenth the "British century," but not so to call the twentieth century the "American century." Of course, the influence of the French and then the British, and the emulation of some of the institutions and habits of their civilizations, went beyond the borders of these great nations; but the impact of the United States upon the world has been wider and perhaps even more decisive. From its very beginning, the United States represented the progress of democracy. The great Alexis de Tocqueville recognized this. His genius saw a change that involved something more than the transition from French and British centuries to an American century, but a change that was coming to France (and to most of the world) after perhaps thousands of years. This was the evolution from aristocratic ages to a democratic one: from ages where minorities ruled to an age where majorities rule (or at least are pretended to rule)—a change in the very structure of history.

The United States was already something like the greatest power in the world in 1914. Then, in 1917, it chose to enter the war in Europe, contrary to its traditions and to the admonitions of some of its Founders. This involved a transformation of its public opinion and of its popular sentiments, from the complexities of American pacifism to American military enthusiasm— and then, soon after the war, to an inclination to turn away from Europe. But meanwhile the American entry into Europe and its consequences were very successful. It decided the war for the Western Allies. Casualties among American soldiers were one-tenth of those suffered by the British and even a smaller fraction of those sustained by the French, who had fought for more than four years and were victors but badly weakened. The prosperity of the United States and the well-being of its people were unequaled after the First World War (as well as after the Second). To explain this by pointing to the natural advantages of the United States—the fact that it is separated from other continents by two of the world's greatest oceans, and that it is an enormous land mass containing enormous national resources—is superficial. Many of the same conditions existed for other Central or South American republics, from Mexico to Argentina. But their political and social histories were, and are, much less significant than those of the United States. Whatever the shortcomings of the latter, the very American conditions of relative liberty, freedom, security, prosperity, and respect for law have been the consequences of what Americans had inherited and adopted from their English-speaking ancestors, many of those legacies prevailing well into the twentieth century. By 1920, Americans of English or Scottish or Irish origin were less than one-fifth of the population of the United States (eighty years before, Tocqueville had still called them "Anglo-Americans"). But the conforming and assimilating power of American customs and institutions was tremendous. It made the power and the prosperity and the prestige of the United States unique. (Such a historical legacy is also apparent in the character of America's northern neighbor, Canada.)

All of this contributed to a large wave of immigration, resumed after the end of the First World War. (This was so of other American republics, too, especially of Brazil and Argentina; the population of the latter increased four- or five-fold after 1880.) But the people and the politicians of the United States, most recently after 1919, chose to shut the "golden door"—not completely, but largely. Two Immigration Acts, in 1921 and 1924, drastically limited immigration to the United States for the first time in the nation's history. There had been popular sentiment against immigration earlier, resulting in minor restrictions that involved mostly the exclusion of actual or potential criminals; but these 1921 and 1924 laws, reflecting American popular sentiment, were born of a national revulsion against Europe (or at least against some Europeans) that began to affect American politics soon after 1918. In a wider and larger sense, they also marked the duality of the American people throughout the next decade. Many Americans—and for some time a considerable majority— believed that their country's involvement in and association with Europe in 1917–1919 had been a mistake. The Republican Party profited from these sentiments and chose as its slogan "Back to normalcy" (an odd word). They repudiated Woodrow Wilson (who suffered a stroke in late 1919) and won a great majority in the presidential election of 1920. The Immigration Acts came in

the election's wake. They established a quota for each nationality of immigrants, strongly restricting those from Eastern and
Southern Europe and granting them but a fraction of the quo-
tas allotted to Western and Northern Europeans, including Germans. There was thus a racial element in these discriminations—
inaccurately but not altogether untruthfully named "isolationism," suggesting the overdue and salubrious isolation of the New
World from the influences and presences of the Old.

American isolationism was of course far from complete. The
Immigration Acts left a number of loopholes. Also, many "iso-
lationists," especially Republicans, were in favor of separating
America from Europe while at the same time promoting the expansion of American military and naval power in the Pacific.
What is more important, these sentiments were largely in accord
with a national tendency to approve of laws governing morality.
This "isolationism" and the legislation of Prohibition—the
attempt to restrict the alcohol consumption of the entire American population—were often supported by the same people.
Throughout the Twenties, the distance between urban America
(especially New York) and rural America, while geographically
and demographically narrowing, remained large and deep (or,
more precisely, very large rather than very deep). At the same
time, the popularity of the Republicans, or of what they seemed
to represent, was decisive. The result was that Americans elected
three Republican presidents in the 1920s: Warren Harding, Calvin Coolidge, and Herbert Hoover—narrow and incompetent,
especially the first two.

Yet the structure of American politics was such that this did
not much matter. After the First World War, what mattered was
the influence of urban America—and not only on rural areas
of the country, but across the world. By 1920, at least three Amer-

ican cities—New York foremost among them, of course—had grown larger than the great capital cities of Europe. More important, they attracted all kinds of Americans, especially writers, journalists, artists, intellectuals, men and women with cosmopolitan aspirations. "Americans are an urban people," wrote the sophisticated Harold Nicolson after his American visit in 1927. (He may have been right then, but not very much longer: suburbanization began to put an end to this urban character after about 1950.) But even more significant was the almost instant spread of American influence all over Europe and in the rest of the world, most recently after 1920. There was no nostalgia anywhere in Europe for the "world of yesterday," for Victorian or Edwardian standards of behavior, much less for their "values." There was a revolution in fashions, especially those of women's clothes, that was unprecedented in modern history (for the first time in centuries, the length of skirts changed not only a few inches up or down, but were diminished by more than one foot). Some of these fashions (including shorter hairstyles for women) originated in America, mostly in New York. All of this was accompanied by a change in the relations between men and women. Much of the same wish to abandon the standards of the past was evident in the arts and literature, and especially in architecture—in huge, modern buildings, largely without ornament, constructed in concrete. There was some reaction to all of this, but only partial and appearing here and there, much later.

These "modern" things influenced and penetrated rural America too. One instrument of their spreading was the automobile, or at least Henry Ford's mass production of them, in the early 1920s. By the end of the decade, two-thirds of American families owned an automobile. It may be argued that the 1920s, in the United States and elsewhere, were not only the first but perhaps the *only* truly Modern Decade (and that the often superficial manifestations of youthful and "revolutionary" changes in the late 1950s and 1960s were hardly anything but further exaggerations of the modernity of the 1920s). An illustration of this was apparent in the American language. In the 1920s, "modern" became an approbatory word throughout America, while "old-fashioned" was deprecatory in almost every sense. A Modern Girl was an all-American girl (while the phrase "modern girl" in Britain and in the rest of Europe had a slightly racy tinge).

The movies largely contributed to this. But perhaps the most telling and enduring evidence of the new, thoughtful, and, yes, sophisticated American contribution to the tastes and culture of the Twenties was American popular music. The overall description of this as "jazz" is misleading. It suggests that the creators of American popular music in the Twenties were African Americans. There had been such an element in American popular sounds and rhythms from the beginning, but the composers of the Twenties were often second-generation Americans, the sons of European immigrants to the United States, and included Americans of older American stock—such as Irving Berlin, George and Ira Gershwin, Jerome Kern, Richard Rodgers, Lorenz Hart, Hoagy Carmichael, Vincent Youmans, and Cole Porter. The quality of their lyrics was not always equal to the elegant rhythms and chords of their music, but the latter were incomparable, appealing to tastes all over the world right up to the present—even though the golden era of that music faded and nearly disappeared after about 1955. The vehicle of their success and popularity, more than films, was the American musical comedy, which for a while was wrongly attributed to the mostly Central European examples of the operetta. A serious—but also necessarily imprecise—exploration of this kind of music would show that most of its best listeners and consumers came from the American upper and urbane classes, even more than from the lower ones (though its best artists and performers were often African Americans). Yet sociological (even more than socio-graphical) categorizations and distinctions among Americans are often imprecise. We may observe that previously—notwith-standing the Immigration Acts of 1921 and 1924, and as a result of some of their special provisions—the 1920s had been marked by an extraordinary arrival of many European musicians, compos-ers, and painters of European and sometimes worldwide repute, along with architects, philosophers, and other intellectuals—an influx perhaps comparable only to the Greek exodus to Rome two thousand years ago. Such crowds of refugees came again during the Hitler age in the 1930s and 1940s (and, after that, dur-ing Stalin's brutal imposition of Communism on much of East-ern Europe). But that first wave (or rather, steady trickle) arrived in the Twenties—an important reason to recognize that despite the temporary popularity of "isolationism," in the 1920s the in-fluence of European culture on the American people (as well as the reverse) was greater than it had been decades before.

Still, this brings us to a nationwide phenomenon—indeed, an essence of America's uniqueness in the 1920s: namely, the incho-ate but enormous extent of the American "middle class." This is a term for a social category that is beginning to lose its meaning in some countries across the world, but—as in other matters—the United States preceded them, particularly in the Twenties. "Mid-dle class" traditionally meant a relatively thin layer between an upper class (largely but not exclusively aristocratic) and the much, much larger lower and lowest classes. But in the United States (and to some extent in Canada, Australia, and New Zea-land), well before the 1920s, the middle class was no longer a "class" but an overall phenomenon. It bulged or ballooned out of the social pyramid and indeed dominated it in many ways. According to one study, by 1927 more than 67 percent (later, 80 percent) of Americans described themselves as "middle class." This was something new and unique in the history of the world, even though such definitions and statistics are necessarily imprecise, since "middle class" is determinable not simply by possessions or income but also by education and by employment in certain professions. Moreover, the European category of "bourgeoisie" was not a very recognizable class or even segment of a class in the United States (even though the word "citizen" in Europe had urban origins, relating to the term "city"). A similar problem is posed by the distinction between the "upper-middle" and "lower-middle" classes; but this was, and is, not unique to the United States. In any event, the United States was not a classless society, even though the category of "class" became less distinct and not immediately or easily recognizable. Meanwhile, many of the habits and customs and even values of most Americans were—somehow—middle class (even though later in the twentieth century "class" and "classy" became approbatory words in the American language).

This kind of near-universality was most apparent, and indeed deeply lodged, in the thoughts and worldview of most Americans. This was their sometimes conscious, or sometimes thoughtless, overall habit of optimism and their belief in "Progress." American optimism—sometimes shallow but also very widespread—was one great difference between most Americans and many Europeans in the Twenties, of course for more than one reason. But perhaps less excusable (or approvable?) was the almost always unquestioned American trust and belief, most of all, in Scientific Progress, going on and on, certainly limitless—a near-universal philosophy, shallow applications of which even appeared in some of the pronouncements of American religious spokesmen and preachers.

In retrospect, one of the amazing features of this optimistic belief was its persistence in America even through the Depression of 1929 and after. Americans are a practical people, and they found it easy and proper to apply their philosophy of Progress to their personal lives and finances. Few people recognized (and not many do, even now) that one of the ingredients of advancing democracy is inflation—of people, of ideas, of valuables, even of money. There was a minor financial crisis at the beginning of the Twenties, but this did not matter. Throughout most of that decade, the prices (and so the assumed values) of almost everything, including real estate, stocks, bonds, and so on, rose (in places, and at times, beyond the bounds of avarice), in tandem with the rise of the "middle class." There was the continuing worldwide prestige of the American dollar, which, as we have seen, had replaced the British pound sterling by 1918 and whose dominance continued, largely unbroken, through and after the Depression and after America's abandonment of the gold standard in 1933. The first sign of real trouble showed up in 1926: the collapse of the Florida land boom—a prototypical and extreme inflation—and the fall in real estate prices there. It should have been a signal, but it hardly caused a ripple elsewhere in the United States. The statements and slogans of successive Republican presidents in the Twenties spurred on the national obsession with Progress. The country's leaders did nothing to warn or admonish their people. (One linguistic remark: "conservative" was a word dismissed and even abhorred by just about all American politicians—until about the mid-1950s.) Then, in October 1929, came a sudden and, here and there, almost precipitous collapse of prices on the New York stock market. There had been similar phenomena in American financial history before, but not of such extent. More important: by 1929, people in the United States were placing their money in stocks to an extent greater than ever before, and greater than anywhere else in the world. The prices did not recover for many years, often not until about a decade later.

Of course this had all kinds of consequences, of which high unemployment was the worst. Yet it is astonishing that it did not much diminish Americans' trust in their country's values. In Europe the Depression was most severe in Germany, where the unemployment rate was comparable to and, here and there, even worse than in the United States. But in Germany, this had grave political consequences (though it is frequently adduced as the main cause of Hitler's rise to power). In America it did not. One indication: the Communist Party of the United States won its largest share of the vote in 1932—but that was a tiny 0.25 percent of the entire electorate (even though a more than considerable number of American intellectuals declared themselves "Communists" in 1932). The great mandate that the American people gave to Franklin Roosevelt in 1932 was, of course, a turning point, even though its financial and economic effects developed relatively slowly during the succeeding years. More telling for this short history of the twentieth century was that the international value of the American dollar hardly changed in the 1930s; and that, even more important, the influence and prestige of the United States did not at all diminish; they went on growing throughout that decade. America and Americans were solid. Perhaps the unthinking habit of optimism and belief in Progress had at least one beneficial effect. The frequent political and social expressions of fear and hatred, evident in some European nations, at least on their extremes, were rare among the American people, decent and tolerant as most of them were.

———————

Two long-range global developments were under way in the 1920s. They had enduring consequences. One of them was that white people gradually ceased migrating to and establishing themselves on other continents. Within the United States itself (also in Canada), the ceaseless movement of people westward (across the "frontier") went on, but in the existing colonies of Britain, France, and the Netherlands, the migration of people from their mother countries to other continents diminished; indeed, in some cases, whites began to return from their colonies. Immigration to South America also tapered off. Yet another consequence was the international spread of the English language, which replaced French as the long-preferred second language of the upper classes. It is at least arguable that one main factor in this was the influence of American movies and American music, part and parcel of the worldwide emulation of America.

6

SOUTH OF THE BORDER
AND ACROSS THE PACIFIC

The Southern Hemisphere—The Far East

HISTORY IS THE RECORD and the memory of mankind. This kind of knowledge is by necessity selective and limited. Such limitation involves the knowledge not only of human beings, but of the globe itself. There were no such terms as "Northern Hemisphere" and "Southern Hemisphere" until men discovered the shape and the dimensions of this earth a few hundred years ago. The Equator, among other things, was a human invention, an abstract circular line. What was not a human invention was the existence of millions of human beings to the south of it, and the slight awareness of them by their northern neighbors. All of this began to change at least six centuries ago. A large migration of white people from the north to the south and west continued into the first half of the twentieth century. Entire continents—including North America, Australia and New Zealand, and parts of South America and southern Africa—had become populated by whites (a reverse movement did not begin until after the Second World War). In 1914, all of Africa was a colony of one or another European state; the only two exceptions were Liberia, at the western edge, and Abyssinia (Ethiopia), on the east of the continent. Sixty years later there remained no European colonial possessions in Africa.

The histories of South and Central America were not as simple as that. In the minds of the first Spanish conquerors who, very soon after Columbus, landed and marched inland in the Caribbean, there was no doubt that these new lands now belonged to them and to Spain. Soon, they vanquished the Aztec and Mayan empires—crushing some of the indigenous peoples or pushing them into the interior of their lands. Spanish colonization was—amazingly—successful in imposing and then perpetuating the rule of the Catholic Church and of the Spanish language on conquered tribal peoples of many kinds. They were —again, somewhat amazingly—largely unable to populate their colonies with more Spanish immigrants. The descendants of the Spanish conquerors found their relations with Spain becoming ever more distant. A consequence of this was that a small ruling class—almost everywhere in Spanish-speaking America, almost always Spanish in race and origin, but also indigenous—wanted to assume control, and wanted to be more and more independent of Spain and of the few Spanish viceroys.

Then, toward the end of the eighteenth century, came the North American and the French revolutions. Their intellectual effect on the overwhelmingly large non-Spanish and nonwhite populations was almost nil—with the exception of an impressive slave revolt led by Toussaint L'Ouverture against the French in Haiti in 1803. But their effect on some of their rulers—especially younger ones in what was still a feudal, not at all middle-class or capitalist, but often militarized, small upper-class society—was more than considerable and perhaps even unavoidable. In Mexico in 1810, and soon thereafter, almost all of the Spanish viceroyalties as far south as Argentina staged rapid revolutions and declared themselves republics. Brazil was an exception, but perhaps only in language: instead of becoming a Spanish colony, that vast piece of the Americas was allotted to Portugal by papal arbitration in 1494, and Brazil remained Portuguese, ruled by an emperor, until 1889.

But throughout the nineteenth century, Brazil's social structure was not very different from that of the other, often small, South and Central American states. By 1830, these republics, "liberated" from Spanish rule by able and ambitious military officers (such as Simón Bolívar, José de San Martín, and Bernardo O'Higgins), had come into existence, transforming the map of the Americas and indeed of the world, essentially where and how they still are today. (The republic of Colombia changed its name from "New Granada" as late as 1860.) Almost all of them started to attract masses of immigrants, especially from southern Italy and the Germanies. This changed the character of the populations of some of them, especially Argentina. Also, like the North Americans, many South and Central Americans went westward and southward, beyond the ever-changing "line" of their own "frontier." But otherwise their histories were very different from those of North America. Almost all of them had a small, slowly growing middle class. (One partial exception was Chile.) In spite of their unequivocal dedication to liberty, freedom, and democracy, they were often ruled by dictators whose tyrannies their peoples accepted, at least for a while. During the nineteenth century, the enormous disparities between the living standards, civilizations, and cultures of the poor and those of the rich hardly diminished. What eventually benefited their populations were the riches of many of their lands and their natural resources. Wheat exports from Argentina, mostly to the British Isles, made that country among the five richest in the world from about 1860 to almost 1930. During that time, British finance, industry, and engineering built many things in Argentina, including its railroads. Yet there was little British immigration to Argentina and little cultural or political influence. As Argentines increasingly emulated and adapted European styles, they looked mainly to France; by 1910, some of their impressive avenues, buildings, and cityscapes resembled those of Paris. (Unlike Brazil, Argentina did not join the United States and Britain during the First World War. It did so very reluctantly at the end of the Second—at a time when much of Argentine popular sentiment had become anti-British.)

But during the twentieth century, there was a gradual transformation in the social structures and the politics of almost all of the Central and South American nations. The slogans, practices, and appeals of populism became ever more important. It may be said that although for the first century of their republican independence, the ideal of most of the Central and South American nations, especially of their educated or middle classes, was Liberty, after about 1910 (this varied from country to country) it became something like Democracy. A result of this was a transitional political period, including plenty of troubles. The worst example was Mexico, which had been defeated by the United States in 1848 and had lost largely uninhabited territories. Its history during the nineteenth century was beset by turmoil and dictatorship. For a short time (during the American Civil War), Mexico acquired an emperor, Maximilian of Habsburg, supported by the French; but in 1867 he, too, was overthrown and murdered, by a local hero, Benito Juárez. (Mussolini's parents gave the hero's name, "Benito," to their newborn son in 1883, a rare example of the Old World emulating something South American. Another was the Argentine tango, which won popularity in Europe in the 1920s.)

Chaos, revolution, and dictatorship became even more frequent in Mexico in the early twentieth century; but there was now a change. The newer demagogues and dictators were populist. Universal manhood suffrage had already existed there for a while, but now an appeal to "the people," for their votes but also beyond, had become dominant. One of the short-lived new presidents, Venustiano Carranza, formulated a fair constitution for Mexico in 1917. He died three years later. By that time, rebellious populists (such as Emiliano Zapata) were gathering enough popular appeal to form revolutionary armies of their own. In 1924 Plutarco Calles, a dictator-president, radical and populist, ascended to power. He saw the Catholic Church as the enemy of Progress and the Mexican people. He fought a bloody three-year war against the "Cristeros," Mexican Catholics ready to defend their faith and their church. In 1930, the conflict died down—somewhat. A single, powerful party, the Partido Revolucionario Institucional (PRI), was founded, and ruled Mexican politics (with various leaders) for the next forty years. Later dictatorships were political rather than military, authoritarian and not totalitarian. This was also true in Brazil, which was ruled by Getúlio Vargas from 1930 to 1945, but with relatively little harm to Brazilian personal and intellectual liberties; in Fulgencio Batista's Cuba; and in Argentina, where José Félix Uriburu was brought to power in 1930 by a military coup, but then gave up his uneven dictatorship two years later. Much of this was due to the growth in the size, prosperity, and political influence of the South and even Central American middle classes. They would increase further during the Second World War, during which most of the leaders of Central America chose to align their foreign and military policies with those of the United States.

During the nineteenth century, the people of the United States and some of their politicians were at times tempted to extend their power southward. But except for the Mexican-American War (1846–1848), this seldom happened. There were occasional instances in which the United States tried to intervene in Cuba, to "liberate" it from Spanish rule and then annex it to the United States (or to the Confederacy of the South, early in the Civil War), but this did not come about. In 1898 the United States chose to declare war against Spain, mostly on the pretext of putting a salutary end to the latest chapter of a Cuban-Spanish civil war. During that "splendid little war," as some American politicians called it, the United States invaded Cuba, acquired Puerto Rico from Spain, and seized Spanish islands in the Pacific; but the long-range effects of the war were more important than the partial intrusion of North America into Central America. Early in the twentieth century, the United States forced the republic of Colombia to cede its northwestern province to American power, where a new republic of Panama was established, including an American zone on both sides of the impressive Panama Canal, the construction of which began in 1903 and was completed in 1915. There were limited interventions by the American military in the repeated Mexican chaos and civil wars, the last of them, quite brief, occurring in 1916. But there was no powerful American political inclination to increase American possessions in the Southern Hemisphere. The more or less secure existence of American material and economic possessions was sufficient. After 1914, the European colonies in South and Central America (a few French, a few minuscule Dutch and Danish islands) would soon cease to exist. More important: the occasional nineteenth-century ambitions of the United States to invade and annex some of Canada had vanished, probably forever.

In the Southern Hemisphere, the mostly British, Irish, and Dutch populations of Australia and New Zealand lived their calm, stolid, pioneer lives throughout the nineteenth and most of the twentieth centuries. The aborigines in these lands were largely powerless. The exception was the Boer War of 1899–1902 between the British and the independence-minded Dutch people in South Africa—a war that the British won, but without drastic or long-range effects. By 1910, all of these former British colonies had autonomous governments and Commonwealth status. In 1914, they stood by the mother country enthusiastically, offering the lives of many thousands of their husbands and sons. The same happened in 1939. But there was a subtle change. More and more, the lives and habits of these descendants of English (and Scottish and Irish) people resembled those of North Americans, rather than those of their ancestors.

Mostly north of the Equator, the stirrings of nationalism (an imprecise term; "anticolonialism" may be a bit more precise) began to appear even before the First World War, or immediately after it. They resulted from the end of the old Ottoman Empire. Turkey, too, became a republic, but with an extraordinary leader —again, a former military officer—Mustafa Kemal, who knew that amputation of weak and useless portions can be as beneficial for an ailing state as for an ailing body. At the same time, he brutally and drastically put an end to the millennial presence of Greek populations in Anatolia, during a brief Greek-Turkish war in 1922–1923. Meanwhile, ancient peoples in the Near East awoke to find themselves citizens of new states such as Syria, Lebanon, Egypt, and Saudi Arabia. For a while, the first two were a French "protectorate," and Egypt was something like a British colony;

but that did not last. Meanwhile, new nationalist dictatorships arose in the Middle East, in Persia (Iran), under Reza Pahlavi, a former Cossack officer and now a shah; or in Afghanistan (under Amanullah Khan), a country never colonized by its powerful neighbors, either by Russia or by Britain from India. A new element was the State of Israel, mostly part of old Palestine, which the British government, for many reasons, declared and established in 1917, under a partial British occupation. Yet the very existence of such a country and its frontiers would lead to long, bitter, and unresolved wars between the Arab and Jewish populations of Israel-Palestine. For thirty years, the British tried to limit Jewish immigration to Israel, until in 1948 they withdrew and the Great Powers recognized the independence of a Jewish state.

After the Second World War, colonialism as practiced by the Western Powers came to an end. (The exception may have been Russia's Central Asian empire, some of it extant even now.) But some of the stirrings of anticolonialism were already evident in the Twenties. In India, there was Mohandas Gandhi, whose humane propaganda on behalf of passive resistance among its people, here and there, impressed all kinds of people across the world. There were anticolonialist speakers and potentially popular leaders in many places in Africa, India, and Indonesia. We must, however, distinguish between nationalism and anticolonialism. Few of the anticolonial states were ethnically homogeneous. They were composed (or, often, uncomposed) of various tribes and various religions—no matter that they now had a national flag, a national government, and established borders. Nationalism was essentially a European (and American) phenomenon and ideology, often conveyed by African and Asian intellectuals to their native peoples from what they saw or learned in Europe or in Britain. Except for a few instances, they did not become important until during and after the Second World War. But meanwhile, something more significant was happening, mostly in Britain. A sympathy for anticolonialism appeared, together with a waning belief in empire. The popular success of works such as E. M. Forster's novel *A Passage to India* (1924) at least suggested and suggests that among the British people, here and there, the Victorian and Edwardian sense of their unique privileges and blessings had weakened.

In the 1920s no Great Power sought further expansion. One exception was Japan. That country had chosen a sort of isolation from the rest of the world; but in the last decades of the nineteenth century, its government and governing classes embarked on a change that was hardly avoidable. In 1868, they had brought about the so-called Meiji reforms, including an extraordinary program of imitating, emulating, and adopting the imperial and technical institutions and achievements of the great world powers. The model for their new army was, by and large, Prussian; for their navy, largely British. By the turn of the century, they were ready for active expansion, first of all across the China Sea. They began to intervene in Korea. In 1894–1895, they fought a naval war against a decrepit Chinese fleet, establishing Japanese rule on some of the islands between China and Japan. Ten years later (1904–1905), they provoked a war with Russia. Their victory was spectacular, at sea as well as on land. Japan's ambitions now tended to spread beyond the islands and ports of China, involving portions of the Far East. (The Treaty of Portsmouth in 1905, mediated by no less a personage than the American president Theodore Roosevelt, allotted to Japan, among other things, the southern half of the Russian island of Sakhalin, close to Siberia.) In 1910, Japan occupied and annexed the old kingdom of Korea. Four years later came the First World War, in which Japan made substantial gains, acquiring a few German colonies in the western Pacific, as well as islands and ports at China's expense. By that time, Japan had a large and very modern navy. In 1920, Japanese ships and troops occupied a portion of the Russian Far East itself, hoping to profit from the chaos of the Russian civil war. Britain and the United States had to recognize the power of Japan. In 1922 the Washington Conference attempted to halt any further division of China. Its naval-disarmament clauses limited the sizes of Japan's battleships. Earlier American popular sympathies for "modern" Japan—many had seen something American in its development—had shifted. As early as 1907, the United States, especially in California, passed regulations virtually prohibiting further Japanese immigration. The older (sometimes religious, other times illusionary) American goodwill toward a defeated and poor Chinese people increased, perhaps in reaction to Japan's aggressiveness. But Japan was now a world power and a world player. By the 1930s there were more automobiles in Japan than in many European countries.

Then, in 1931, Japan began to push into the Chinese mainland, with the aim of making that vast and ancient country into something like Japan's junior partner, or even a satellite. A history of China—because of its stunning length and complexity—poses great problems for historians, whether Chinese or foreign. The history of Chinese rulers and of their power—that is, political and military history, the prime interest at least for most general historians—is difficult to reconstruct. Chinese trade with Europe and with America, as well as the West's knowledge of and taste for Chinese goods and art, was evident for many centuries. The relatively open approach to China, and the weakness of its central governments, inspired some of the Great Powers, even though oceans away, to establish their own small enclaves and ports on the China Sea (called "capitulations," in the international law of those days), beginning with the British in Hong Kong in the 1840s, and followed, in different ways, by French, Russians, and Germans. Then the Japanese started to surround China by occupying Korea and beginning to penetrate, in various ways, into the rich portions of the northeastern Chinese Empire.

This, among other important matters, contributed to the Chinese Revolution in 1912. In a few days, China became a republic and its ruling dynasty disappeared. As in many other colonial countries, the movers of such a revolution were intellectuals who knew something of the world, as well as ambitious military generals. One of the latter was Yuan Shih-kai, who two years later proclaimed himself a new emperor, but soon thereafter died. More enduring and impressive were the prestige and power of Sun Yat-sen, American-educated and a Christian (as were other such leaders of the 1912 revolution, to whom Christianity also meant something "Western"). It is both remarkable and impressive that Sun Yat-sen (who died in 1925) has been venerated and idolized by *both* of the subsequent Chinese leaders and soon enemies: Mao Tse-tung, a Communist, and Chiang Kai-shek, an anti-Communist. (Chiang, a Christian, married Sun Yat-sen's daughter.) In 1926–1927, inspired by Sun Yat-sen, Chiang attempted to establish the first national, unitary, and effective Chinese government by a national party, the Kuomintang. The Communists and Mao Tse-tung challenged and revolted against him in 1927. Chiang beat him, and Mao and his cohorts had to flee to a remote northwestern region of China, where Mao received minimal Russian support. Chiang became a beneficiary of first political, then material, and finally military support from the United States, a decade or so later.

By that time, some of the leaders of Japan, especially those of the imperial navy and army, decided that the time had come for Japan to extend its rule over China further—even at the risk of a possible war with the United States (a war they wrongly thought would be limited to the far western Pacific and the Far East). In 1931 the Japanese army occupied the vast, rich, and for centuries China-bound province of Manchuria, establishing a Japanese satellite state, a Manchurian kingdom. Japan was condemned by the League of Nations in Geneva, and withdrew from it without a thought. The next year, they were in control of the ancient Chinese capital, Peking (Beijing). Chiang moved his national government to Nanking. In 1937, the Japanese-Chinese war started, full scale. In 1940, Japan chose to be an ally of Germany. By then, China had become *the* principal problem between Japan and the United States.

Yet the Second World War broke out in Europe, as had the First.

7

"MIDDLE CLASS" IS
NOT "BOURGEOIS"

The failure of liberal democracies—Authoritarian governments, dictatorships—A crisis of capitalism—The United States and other examples of parliamentary democracy

IN NOVEMBER 1918 there was a widespread opinion that the victory of the Western Allies also meant the defeat, perhaps enduring, of imperial and nondemocratic states, such as Germany and its allies. This perspective was dear to the American people, and particularly to their president, Woodrow Wilson—who, in March 1917, took great comfort from the news of the liberal revolution in Russia and the abdication of the tsar, which relieved the United States and the Western democracies of the burden of being allied with an imperial state. We know that soon thereafter liberalism and parliamentarism in Russia were trampled down by the Bolshevik Communists. But what we ought to consider now is the failure of liberal democracy in most of Europe, contrary to the expectations of many people in 1918 and for a brief time thereafter.

The end of the war *seemed* to many people, in many nations, the triumph of liberalism and democracy—perhaps even more of liberalism than of democracy—as they were represented by

Britain and France. A consequence of this was that they were emulated, as well, in countries that were not among the victors. In 1919, nearly all of the new and old states of Europe had liberal parliamentary governments. That did not last long. One reason for this was the gradual, though more and more evident, decline of the influence of Britain and France in the affairs of Europe. A deeper though less recognized element was the growing unpopularity of bourgeois values.

This may call for a short explanation. We have seen that the First World War (unlike either the French revolutionary war or the Napoleonic wars) inspired very little or no nostalgia for the restoration of erstwhile standards and values. Here and there, such a tendency went together with skepticism about the very principles of the eighteenth-century, mainly French, Enlightenment. We must at least consider that the Enlightenment and its consequences were embraced and supported primarily by the growing middle classes and by their upper strata, the so-called "bourgeoisie" (not quite identical with "middle class"). Relevant here is the disdainful meaning and employment of the adjective "bourgeois" after about 1920, and not only by Communists or other votaries of the Left. This was particularly so in Germany, and also among all kinds of intellectuals.

In much of Europe, especially in its south and east (the latter encompassing at least six or seven new states after 1918), the so-called middle classes and especially their bourgeois upper strata were sparse and weak. So was the historical and popular appeal of many of their institutions, such as parliaments (and liberalism). Most everywhere—and especially in the new states— the composition of governments and parliaments did not reflect the composition of their nations: the former consisted mostly of middle-class people, universal manhood suffrage notwithstanding. Sooner or later, a dislike of such a liberal system, or lack of system—an antipathy that attributed the frequent examples of inefficiency and corruption to the governing classes—began to appear, not only on but also beneath the surface of politics.

The result was the rise of new dictatorships which, oddly enough, were not unlike those in some of the states of South America, though they neither were inspired by nor emulated the latter. In 1922, Mussolini and his Fascist legions marched into Rome. In 1923, the king of Spain gave a military general, Miguel Primo de Rivera, near-dictatorial powers. In 1926, in Portugal, António Salazar, a serious and respectable professor, became the authoritarian head of government. In the same year, the liberal parliamentary powers of the government of Poland were reduced by the partial dictatorship of Marshal Józef Piłsudski, a hero of the Polish nation in 1918 and 1920. In 1927, 1929, and 1934, the liberal parliamentary governments of Lithuania, Latvia, and Estonia were transformed, more or less like most of the other states of Eastern and Central Europe.

In every one of these countries, the unpopularity of liberalism preceded the establishment of their new regimes, for which "dictatorships" is a necessarily imprecise term. "Authoritarian," and not "totalitarian," would be more accurate ("totalitarian" is a vague and often misleading adjective, even when applied to the lives of entire nations such as those under Hitler and Stalin). Authoritarian was less than "total" because these new regimes chose to maintain some of their older institutions, such as parliaments (though limiting their powers and establishing, in some cases, one-party rule; in Spain, Italy, Yugoslavia, Romania, Albania, Bulgaria, and Greece, they respected—and in some states even confirmed—their monarchies, the highest powers of the state). They also, *mutatis mutandis,* maintained considerable in-

tellectual freedoms. Another detail: these authoritarian dictatorships were the result not of revolutions but of coups d'état (a term
for which, fortunately, there is no English equivalent: overnight
changes in the occupation and possession of government buildings). They had not much in common with Hitler and with National Socialism. But to the abovementioned cases we may add
Austria, which by 1931–1932 had given what remained of parliamentary liberalism or even democracy and had instituted authoritarian rule. In Hungary, too, under the near-monarchical
rule of Admiral Miklós Horthy (the "Regent"), the parliament
remained, though suffrage was still limited. At that time, there
were serious observers and even statesmen in the democratic
countries, too, who thought and occasionally said that the existence of such regimes might be a way to the future, given the
more or less impractical rule of liberal and parliamentary governments.

   An example of this is the reputation (and the achievements) of
Mussolini. He was a Socialist who recognized the meaningless-
ness of international socialism, together with the appeal of nationalism; he broke with the Socialist Party in 1915, went to war
in the trenches, and in 1919 started to form a new party or movement called "Fascism," a term derived from the Latin word *fas-
ces,* meaning a bundle of reeds tied together—a symbol of authority in ancient Rome. His party had something like storm
troopers, wore black shirts, were energetic proponents of order
and law, and so on. This filled a vacuum—or even more than a
vacuum—in Italy, where public order and the reputation of governments were riven by frustration and, at times, near-chaos.
The upper and middle classes were relieved by Mussolini's program, which seemed to be nationalist rather than radical (the
Communists had made a few inroads among the working classes

in and before 1923). Mussolini asserted his respect for the monarchy and for its institutions; conversely, the king, Victor Emmanuel III, accepted and even respected him. There were some ugly episodes, including murders, perpetrated by a few brutal Fascists, but they were soon forgotten. By 1926, Mussolini ruled atop a one-party state. But compared to other authoritarian dictatorships, he went further. His plan was to change the old bourgeois parliamentary system into a unified national assembly where the men elected would not represent different parties, but would be chosen from the ranks of their professions and occupations. This was the ideal of a corporate state, which was subsequently emulated elsewhere, too; yet, even in Italy, it did not really become complete. Nevertheless, it behooves us to pay some attention to it, since it represented Mussolini's overall ambition—indeed, his worldview—which was that one must strengthen the state above all. This was especially relevant to Italy, which was not a unified state until about 1870 and where regional differences and local authority continued to exist. After 1926, there was increasing evidence showing that Mussolini's militarist inclinations were even more dominant than his otherwise often successful domestic programs of reform. He began to appear more and more frequently in military uniform. His main motto, repeated over and over to university students, was "Libro e moschetto": "Book and rifle." That his plan to make Italians a military (and race-conscious) people was an almost complete failure would become evident soon after he made Italy enter the Second World War in 1940. But that was still a decade away.

Meanwhile his reputation grew, almost sensationally, and not only within Italy. After all, even under his rule Italy remained a civilized country with considerable private freedoms, artistic achievements, traditional pleasures, functioning institutions, and not a few intellectual liberties. His Lateran Treaty with the Holy See in 1929 put an end to the long centuries of quarrels and even occasional hostilities between the Vatican and the Italian state. Throughout the world, most Catholics and especially their hierarchies admired Mussolini almost unconditionally throughout the 1930s. His reputation radiated beyond Italy, beyond religion, and even beyond politics. Italy's former traditional enemy Austria (and Hungary) sought his support and alliance in and after 1927. Winston Churchill visited him and expressed his respect for him a few years later. "What we need is a Mussolini," said not a few American congressmen and politicians. Here and there, emulating Mussolini and Italy, Fascist parties came into existence—surprisingly, in 1931 in England, where Fascism had a small but not inconsiderable following in the 1930s.

None of this would last. And the same was true of most other authoritarian dictatorships, up to and during the Second World War, when Hitler overshadowed Mussolini (the reverse of their relationship in the Twenties), and Mussolini and Italy became Hitler's satellites; by 1938, National Socialism had become more powerful and universal than Fascism. Mussolini could have avoided this—perhaps. But such was not his character.

―――――――――

We must now, in this short history of the twentieth century, depart from Central, Southern, and Eastern Europe in order to sum up something that, even to the present day, is considered by many people as the gravest and deepest event experienced by almost all of the world around 1930: the Great Depression, or, as some people thought, the Crisis of Capitalism. These two terms—as well as their consequences—overlap; but to sharpen my argument, I ought to deal with the second before the first.

For long decades, many people thought (or were told) that the great struggle of their times was the worldwide struggle between Capitalism and Communism; and that later, in the twentieth century, these great ideas and their institutions were almost inevitably represented and even incarnated by the United States and the Soviet Union. This view, though encompassing history and much of the world, was shortsighted and wrong. (I must postpone dealing with this until Chapter 12, which focuses on the origins of the so-called "Cold War.") But these considerations of Capitalism and Communism well preceded the Second World War and its consequences; and therefore I must, necessarily, briefly sum up the very shortcomings of the word "Capitalism" itself and apply it to the history of the 1920s and 1930s.

There have been rich people and poor people since the beginning of time, just as there were, I dare to imagine, bankers and indigents. Yet the words "Capitalism" and "Communism" appeared, at least in English, only around the middle of the nineteenth century. One problem with Capitalism was (and is) that although there were capitalists, it was never an Ism. (The trouble with Communism, too, is that although there were and still are people and governments that call themselves Communist, international Communism, since even before 1989, has been a Wasm.) Capitalists were often sure of themselves, but did not think much about whether they incarnated an ideology or not. What was true in the nineteenth century, as well as before and after, is how much money and finance mattered. Property, especially when valued in monetary terms, gave people security even more than before; and money paid interest and gave security. Even more remarkable—historically, that is—is the extent to which solid money, all kinds of money, remained secure until 1914. The value of national monies, or call them currencies, remained largely the same for decades, even after revolutions and wars. But meanwhile, the democratization of much of the Western world continued, bringing about, among other things, an increasing consciousness especially of the working classes. A result of this was the growing dissatisfaction with great social and economic inequities and the belief that it was the duty of a government and a nation to provide laws and regulations to improve, at least somewhat, the economic and living conditions of its poorer classes—for the sake of national unity, but also for the sake of avoiding bitter class wars: social revolutions. The radical proponents of the elimination of gross social injustices were the Socialist parties, appearing well before 1900 and gaining popular support, often through elections. A more radical and dogmatic version of the Socialists became the Communists, who believed —wrongly—that classes were more important than nations, that what mattered were states, not nations, and that the aim of humanity ought to be Communist states governing all of the means of production. That was one, but only one, of the myopic follies of Marx, confusing nations and states—indeed, paying hardly any attention to the former.

What happened in 1914 and after should have demonstrated the shallowness and the folly of such beliefs and dogmas. Communists and Socialists, and many Liberals and most Progressives who believed that classes were more important than governments—that the international sympathies of working classes across states and nations would be decisive, even to the extent of making wars impossible—were entirely wrong. A British or French worker felt nothing in common with his German or Austrian counterpart; indeed, the patriotic convictions and enthusiasms of the working classes were, perhaps, even stronger than ever. (The fact that after the war Socialist and Communist parties and intellectuals survived this obvious bankruptcy of their predictions is another story, perhaps indicative of how slowly ideas change, even in the twentieth century.) Still, by 1930 Social Democratic parties and their ideas were retreating almost all over Europe. But so, too, was international Capitalism—except, as said above, it was not an Ism. Indeed, the meaning and the use of the term "Capitalism," perhaps especially in the United States, had been inflated beyond reason; to millions, it meant the sacredness and the preservation of personal property, endangered by their vicious and godless opponents, the Communists.

Yet by 1930 an economic and financial crisis had developed swiftly throughout most of the Western world. It was less destructive and decisive than it seemed for a long time—we may assert this in retrospect; but even though rich men and "capitalists" remained, as they always will remain, we may assert that nineteenth-century "classic" Capitalism had come to an end. For its principal pillar was solidity, enduring solidity. That solidity required the solidity of money. It is amazing how little the value of national currencies changed before 1914. The same was largely true of the prices of precious metals, foremost of gold. Banknotes and paper money almost entirely replaced the circulation of gold before 1914, but their repute was due to the overall trust in the gold standard, since anyone calling at a bank could require that a sum be paid to him in gold, silver, or paper. (Yet even before 1914, few people made this kind of choice—though the monetary gold standard had become more and more abstract.)

In 1931, Great Britain suddenly announced the abandonment of the gold standard for the purpose of supporting the pound. The United States, under Roosevelt, did the same in early 1933.

There is a serious minority of thoughtful economists who state, even now, that this meant the end of Capitalism, with infinitely dangerous consequences, including persistent inflation. Perhaps true, but not true enough. The same applies to the entire long-range view of the 1930s Depression. It brought deplorable conditions and consequences. But these did not endure. Following the New York stock market crash in October 1929, banks went bankrupt and had to close in the United States and, worse, in Europe. There was, for the last time in the twentieth century, deflation, meaning that prices were falling; but much more dangerous was rising unemployment, especially in the United States and in Germany, reaching a peak in 1932–1933. Then, under Roosevelt and especially Hitler, but also in most other countries, this began to recede—rapidly in Germany, more gradually in the United States, where most of the phenomena of the Great Depression came to an end by the conclusion of the Thirties. By that time, all money was issued by governments; and people have accepted this, as well as gradual inflation, ever since. And even the quickest and most superficial look at most of the world since the 1930s ought to show us how, during the rest of the twentieth century, the possessions and the relative security and prosperity of large numbers of people grew, often amazingly—if not "beyond the dreams of avarice," then surely beyond the speculations of all economists and political scientists of the 1930s. It is true that much of this has been made possible by the enormous availability of credit to all kinds of people. (In the nineteenth century, credit had been a prerogative of men who already possessed considerable capital. What may happen to credit in the twenty-first century, I cannot tell.)

Strangely, the obvious sufferings and pessimism fueled by the Great Depression of the early 1930s did not lead to revolutions or

other political upheavals. Those who attributed Hitler's coming
to power in 1933 to the Depression were wrong. Nor did Communist and Socialist parties gain much of a following during the
Depression; the main example of this was the United States. The
parliamentary, legalistic, and still quite liberal political system of
the United States survived the Depression without much damage
or even much change. One indication of this is the American
people's rejection of extreme political parties. Except for a few
conventicles of radicals and intellectuals, there was no sign that
Americans at large—even though so many of them had lost their
employment during the Depression—had much or any inclination to question the existence of their traditional (two-party) political system. Had the Depression continued and gotten worse,
this would not have happened; but that was not to be. The election of Franklin Roosevelt to the presidency in November 1932,
along with his inauguration the following March, was a turning
point. Instantly he instilled confidence in the American people.
His economic and social programs differed little from those of
Hoover, his predecessor and opponent. But that scarcely mattered, or mattered not at all. His confidence, shining from his impressive face, was radiant. First his financial, then his economic
and social reforms such as the New Deal, came, step by step; but
the overall impression, dear to the ears of the American people,
was the kind of confidence of which Roosevelt had plenty. He
had his political rivals—interestingly, as in Europe, on the Right
and not on the Left—American demagogues and populists such
as Huey Long of Louisiana and Father Coughlin, the radio priest;
but by Roosevelt's second and most impressive electoral triumph
in 1936, Long was gone and the radio priest was told to talk less
and less. In the eyes of the rest of the world, American democracy was solid, like the American dollar.

Not all of this, but much of it, was the same in the remaining parliamentary and social democracies of the world: Australia, New Zealand, Canada, and Ireland, the stolid democracies of Northwestern Europe, the Scandinavian kingdoms and states, and Holland and Belgium. In almost all of them there arose "Fascist" parties and movements in 1932, but these did not get very far. Despite their shortcomings—and there were many—the Swedish, Dutch, Danish, and other people were neither ready nor inclined to upset or transform their accustomed institutions, uninspiring or not very effective though they may have been. So the Fascist parties lived on, some of them even under German occupation, through the Second World War. This was, and remains to their credit, even though their situation was not as simple as that.

8

"I WAS A NATIONALIST,
BUT I WAS NOT A PATRIOT"

National Socialism—Hitler

NATIONAL SOCIALISM, OR CALL it nationalist socialism, has been the great political phenomenon of the twentieth century—and beyond. The end of the Second World War, the death and disappearance of Adolf Hitler, diminished its appeal for a short time, but did not extinguish it at all. Unlike Communism, nationalist socialism is not a Wasm. In some countries, especially in Europe, more or less openly nationalist socialist parties win about 20 percent in national elections now, more than three-quarters of a century after Hitler killed himself. Still, in this brief history of the twentieth century, I must attempt to describe the rise of National Socialism in its heyday, and its association with the greatest (and most demonic) figure in the entire history of an entire century.

But before that, most of my readers must face, or admit, a strange and unusual problem—namely, the uneasiness, the confusion, and the consequent shortcomings of the categorization of nationalist socialism, even now. Most people (including commentators) describe or refer to its parties and spokesmen as members of the extreme Right. This will not do. Among other things, it suggests that National Socialists and National Socialism were and are reactionary—but this is not at all true. They had (and have) nothing to do with the Old Right; they had nothing to do with conservatism. As a matter of fact, their most determined and principled opponents were often men of the Right rather than of the Left.

Searching for a more precise category, many people, even now, affix the adjective "Fascist" to National Socialism—another mistake. Mussolini's main purpose was to strengthen the unity and power of the Italian state. Hitler (on more than one occasion) said that the state was a *Zwangsform,* a constrained framework: what mattered was not the state but the *Volk,* the nation. Although there were other differences between the two leaders, they became allies, and Mussolini and Fascism adopted more of the characteristics of National Socialism. (So would Stalin.)

"Definitions are tricks for pedants," Samuel Johnson was supposed to have said; but the histories of words and of their widespread usages are not. Here we come to the fourth adjective customarily affixed especially to German National Socialism: "Nazi" —almost a pun, but more precise than the abovementioned terms. The word enables us to point out the ways in which international socialists and even Social Democrats differed from the German *nationalist* socialists and their party around 1920–1921. The full term was "Nazi-Sozi"—that is, socialists of a national variety. We have seen that the "Sozi" half of this hyphenated term disappeared, tellingly so. The designation "Nazi" meant much more than "Sozi." So "Nazi" remained.

From the very beginning of Socialist parties and movements, they had members and supporters who were opponents of internationalism. (This is one problem with rigid categorization; consider, for example, the British Labour Party, which shied away from internationalism while often eschewing the adjective "Socialist.") In the late 1870s in Germany, the largest Socialist party in Europe adopted the name "Social Democrats," meaning that the party preferred to prosper through democratic and parliamentary—not revolutionary—means. But this is not our concern now. Almost from the very beginning of Socialism in Europe, there were people who were repelled by the materialism, the class-conflict slogans, the anti-Christian rhetoric, and the internationalist programs and components of the Socialist parties and some of their leaders ("stateless bandits" some people called Socialists). Soon, Christian Socialist parties appeared: "Christian" nationalists and populists who insisted on their opposition to "international" and godless Socialists and Social Democrats. Especially in Austria and Germany, their influence and the size of their voters increased. In some nations they were anti-Semitic; in others, not.

Determinedly and categorically, the German National Socialist party was anti-Jewish. This appeared almost immediately after the First World War. It was a minor party during the Twenties, especially during the relatively peaceful and democratic interlude (1924–1930) between the two world wars. In 1928, it attracted fewer than 3 percent of German voters. By September 1930, its membership had grown to almost 19 percent. In the two elections in 1932, it was nearly twice that size. This had something to do with the Depression, including the very high unemployment rate in Germany; but that was (and remains) an insufficient explanation for such a success. The German Nazi Party, almost alone among all other parties, had no real economic program. Its appeal to many Germans, including large segments of the working classes, was something else. It was nationalist and populist, anti-foreign and anti-Semitic. But its popularity was not separate from the work of its extraordinary spokesman and leader, Adolf Hitler.

———————

There exist entire libraries dealing with Hitler (some of them, I hope, include my singular book *The Hitler of History*). He alone caused the Second World War—a war that, unlike much of the First, spread worldwide; a war during which more people than in the First, including many millions of civilians, died or were murdered; a war that lasted longer than the First; and a war with tremendous and enduring consequences. This section will be limited to his career well before the war, when this lonely and entirely unknown young man suddenly decided to enter politics, at first with dubious results. But then, fourteen years later, he rose to become the chancellor of Germany, supported by many kinds of people—and by the majority of all Germans.

He was not a "German." He was born in Austria (in a town close to the German border), but then he, like a fair number of Austrians, was uninspired, to say the least, with citizenship in an ancient monarchy, a multinational empire. He phrased this clearly and succinctly in one pithy sentence in his otherwise long-winded book, *Mein Kampf* (*My Struggle*), written mostly when he was in prison in 1924: "I was a nationalist, but I was not a patriot." Patriotism and nationalism: how often these words are confused and their true meanings obscured in our own times. Yet—especially in Austria—their distinctions were more evident, at least in the first portion of the twentieth century. A nationalist was an Austrian whose main affection was to Germandom and to Germany. Nationalism could be (and usually was) aggressive and—at least potentially—revolutionary; patriotism was defensive, old-fashioned, and traditionalist. No use parsing these adjectives further. But this is what they meant (and still mean), in more than one way.

Hitler did not speak much during the first thirty years of his life. He read enough; and from the fragmentary evidence we have, he shared the views of, or was influenced by, the pro-German nationalists—but they had no great effect on his life then. He moved from Austria to Munich in 1913, and in spite of his Austrian citizenship, he volunteered for the German army and served in a Bavarian regiment in August 1914. His military record was more than respectable—that of a brave and even self-effacing soldier. In the very last months of the war, he suffered a crisis. He was injured by a cloud of poison gas and sent to a hospital. There, he learned the news of Germany's surrender. He was stunned, and struck in his innermost heart. As he wrote in *Mein Kampf*, at that moment "I decided to be a politician"—strange choice for a man almost thirty years old, and until then tight-lipped, largely silent about his thoughts. For once, it seems, he said nothing but the truth.

That, too, changed before long, and how . . . It took about another half-year before Hitler realized his gift for speaking, and then for public speaking. Shortly before Winston Churchill died, John F. Kennedy said that Churchill had "mobilized the English language." It may not be an exaggeration to say that Adolf Hitler "mobilized" popular, common German language. Of course, Churchill in 1940 called forth something old—English pride—whereas Hitler appealed to something relatively new: a German feeling for vengeance. As early as 1921, Hitler said: "Hate! We are blessed with hate!" He kept saying that. Within three years, this unknown, forlorn, undistinguished, ex-soldier became the leader of the NSDAP (Nationalsozialistische Deutsche Arbeiter-partei), the German National Socialist Workers' Party. This leadership and his public-speaking ability went hand in hand. In November 1923, he and his party decided they were strong and powerful enough to lead a nationalist revolution that, radiating from Munich, would spread across most of Germany within a week, perhaps even days. At the head of the party militia, Hitler marched toward the center of the city, often cheered on by jubilant crowds. But the conservative authorities of Munich chose to stop him. Police bullets struck a few of his followers. Hitler fell to the ground with a badly wrenched arm. Eventually, he was imprisoned and brought to trial. There, he outshouted and outmaneuvered some of his judges. He wrote or dictated *Mein Kampf* mostly when in prison. In another year, he was free.

He also recognized—all of his "revolutionary" rhetoric notwithstanding—that Germans did not like real revolutions; that he and his National Socialist Party must eventually rise to power through other means, probably even elections. In 1926, there were no indications that this could succeed. The popularity of the party did not increase until 1930. It is significant that through those years, Hitler's confidence remained largely unshaken. Even in 1932–1933, when support for the National Socialists rose sharply, some of his cleverest followers, such as Joseph Goebbels and Hermann Goering, doubted whether Hitler could ever come close to power. Hitler himself had no doubts at all. On January 30, 1933, his confidence was justified. Field Marshal Paul von Hindenburg, once a war hero and now president of Germany, received Hitler and handed him Germany's chancellorship.

It is lamentable to record that much of this was due to German conservatives and to their parties in 1933. In and after 1930, the tone of Hitler's demagogic rhetoric abated somewhat. This was part and parcel of his realization that his appeal to the German middle classes had risen and was rising. Before 1923, he and the NSDAP tried their best (and worst) to recruit followers from the working classes. In 1932–1933 their propaganda (or at least some of it) began to influence the German middle classes. Consequently, some of their parties, associations, and leaders began to consider some kind of coalition with Hitler. The prime example of this tendency was Franz von Papen, a clever but sinuous and shallow potential statesman. In July 1932 he became, for a few months, chancellor of Germany. Some of his decisions during his chancellorship were meant to restrict and injure the German Left but not the Right. This was in accord with his belief—or rather, with his vision of history, which many other German conservatives shared—that what was happening in Germany now was the very reversal of the slogans (and ideals) of the French Revolution of one hundred and fifty years earlier: that 1933 meant the end of the era of 1789. Papen and his kind also thought they would be able to control, limit, and soon marginalize Hitler, who, after all, was indebted to them for suggesting his chancellorship to Hindenburg. The very opposite was soon to happen. Hitler's first cabinet NSDAP ministers were a minority, but not for long.

In less than a few months, Hitler energetically and brutally assumed near-total power in Germany—and through parliamentary elections, from which only one party, the Communist Party, was excluded. Thus the so-called Third Reich was born. The solitary soldier (corporal, to be more exact), who assumed the leadership of what eventually became the largest political party in Germany, now began to show his statesmanlike capacities. His ability to rule may have sprung from his extraordinary (and at times near-diabolic) insight into the weaknesses of people, including people of utterly different classes and nations. He also realized the overall priority of nationalism over socialism: among other things, the titans of German industry and finance were no more obstacles in his way than were the sometimes cowed politicians of the Social Democratic Party in 1933. When someone asked him the following year whether and when he planned to nationalize the great German industries, he responded: "Why should I nationalize the industries? I am nationalizing the people."

We are not yet done with Hitler. Still to come was the Second World War, in which he was the dominant factor, more than his party and National Socialism. But I began this chapter with the latter, arguing that we have not yet come to the end of it, evidence of this being the still confused and confusing categorization of National Socialism, often with wrong designations affixed to it. At times, this was conscious, as in the case of Stalin. Throughout the Great War and after, Stalin forbade the use of the term "National Socialist"—always, he spoke of "Hitlerites" or "Fascists." A reason for this should not be hard to detect. It was obvious to him that his rule and program and policy for his Soviet Union was nationalist, more and more so; and that for all kinds of reasons, such a term ought to be omitted. In addition, he came to admire Hitler (this sympathy was more than reciprocal, since Hitler also came to admire Stalin). This we know not from official texts and public rhetoric, but from all kinds of evidence in their own words. Like Mussolini, Stalin learned much from Hitler—further evidence of the near-universality of nationalist socialism.

More than two-thirds of a century after 1945, there are still national socialist parties (and believers) in many nations throughout the world. The existence (mostly in Europe) of Social Democratic parties notwithstanding, the adjective "socialist" has lost much of its meaning. The reason for this is that, in our democratic age, every government has adopted the social practices of the "welfare state," including at least the protection of its relatively poorest elements, together with numberless other practices beyond the daydreams of Socialists at the beginning of the twentieth century. The now relatively small but not inconsiderable national socialist parties are xenophobic and even anti-Semitic. Whether in the twenty-first century nationalism will become ever stronger, I cannot tell.

Two oddities remain worth mentioning and considering. One is that almost everywhere in the world (and not only in Germany), the flags and colors and symbols of most things of the National Socialist regimes and parties before 1945, such as swastikas, are strictly forbidden—as if they were still toxic and dangerous, three generations and two-thirds of a century after the suicide of Hitler. Communist symbols and other Communist insignia are still allowed here and there. Is this perhaps another indication that the latter is a Wasm, whereas National Socialism is not? Another curious (or perhaps not very curious) oddity is that while the latter is openly or indirectly praised for some of the achievements of the National Socialist era, even the most vocal or extreme National Socialist parties and their leaders and spokesmen never, never mention Hitler. Have they rejected or are they rejecting him? There are reasons to doubt that. Or is he still too dangerous, too hot to handle?

9

THE WAVE OF THE FUTURE

The Hitler decade—His domination of Europe—The coming of the Second World War

EVEN BEFORE THE Second World War began, Hitler came to rule much of Europe. He had thought that he could achieve even more—that he could dominate most of Europe without a war. The war then showed that his abilities as a determined and often brutal statesman were matched—well, often—by his capacities as a military leader. Blind he was not. All of his pronouncements and extreme decisions notwithstanding, he did not want a big war. This we know from his disappointment when the news came on September 3, 1939, that, after all, Britain and France had chosen to declare war against Germany. He knew that the British and the French had done this reluctantly. He knew that all through the 1930s his potential opponents, including even the Great Powers, had not confronted him—for all kinds of reasons, primarily because they wanted to avoid a second world war.

We must consider, too, another of his limits. Many of his opponents thought and said that he wanted to rule the world. No: he wanted to rule most of Europe (and realize all the advantages that would accrue to his Germany as a matter of course). To rule Europe was enough, perhaps even more than enough. But there was yet another constraint that made him push forward—if need be, at the cost of a great war: he believed that time was against him. This was not so. In 1939, even his often impetuous friend Mussolini wrote to tell him this was not so, that he need not hurry. This was perhaps Adolf Hitler's greatest mistake. The result was a second world war—but at what cost!

The 1930s were his decade; but 1934 was not his best year. How he consolidated his power—and prestige and reputation—within a twelvemonth in Germany was (and remains) amazing. But he convinced himself that he had to get rid of most of his potential opponents. On June 30, 1934, his secret-police minions murdered hundreds of men, some of them from within his own party, the others not (including General Kurt von Schleicher, Hitler's predecessor as chancellor, killed together with his wife). It did not matter. What mattered, lamentably so, is that the most conservative and respectable elements in Germany—the army and the churches, including even a few leaders of the Catholic Church, after June 30 went on to respect and admire Hitler.

He had a small setback in 1934 in his foreign policy. This involved Austria, where the National Socialist party and its adherents were growing ever stronger. In July of that year, some of them rose in rebellion against the Catholic-conservative regime of the Austrian chancellor, Engelbert Dollfuss. Dollfuss was not a Leftist, not a Liberal, not a Democrat; in February 1934, he had crushed the Austrian Social Democrats, a not inconsiderable party, with cannons and guns. A Nazi he was not. On July 25, some of the Austrian Nazis rose up, broke into the Chancellery, and killed Dollfuss. Yet the Austrian police and army came up and the Nazi conspirators were defeated. Even now it is unclear whether they had been not merely inspired but supported or urged on by Hitler; it seems they were not. In any event, it was a setback for him. Even Mussolini made noises and moved some of the Italian army close to the Austrian border.

Hitler's setback was temporary. He was beginning to dismantle the Versailles Treaty. Germany was to be rearmed, with shining new means and results. In 1935 the British government chose to sign a naval rearmament treaty with Germany, not at all unfavorable to the latter—but then Hitler's navy was the least important of his armed forces. In Nuremberg he dictated new laws excluding Jews (on a racial basis) from anything like German citizenship. He wanted to expel them from Germany. Now he prepared for his most daring move, which was the cancellation of the "nonmilitarized" status of the western Rhineland. That was a strategic change of great importance. Well after the Versailles Treaty, a democratic and pro-Western government of Germany agreed with the Western Powers, first of all with France, that there would be no German military installations on the west bank of the Rhine, across the French frontier. (The French had added—or thought they had added—to their security by building the so-called Maginot Line, an array of impressive fortresses containing heavy artillery along their frontier with Germany.) On March 6, 1936, Hitler decreed and ordered the remilitarization of the western Rhineland. Thereby, he instantly abolished that most important element for the security of France (and Belgium) in the event of a war with Germany.

This was his biggest gamble up to that point—and he succeeded. The reactions of the French government, the one most directly affected, were feeble. They depended on the British, and the British chose not to do anything. I shall have to return to Britain in the Thirties; but before that, we must realize that the tendency to come to terms with Hitler's Germany now began to influence entire governments—and peoples—throughout Europe, indeed throughout the world. What Hitler and the Third Reich represented seemed to be something like the wave of the future. The Olympics, staged in Berlin in 1936, were a shining example of it. But all of this went beyond semblances, images, reputations. Mussolini decided to join Hitler. Hence the so-called Rome-Berlin Axis was born. In Mussolini's case, this was more than a politic or strategic calculation. He was convinced that the bourgeois democracies, the remnant powers of Western Europe, including even Britain, were at, or at least close to, the end of their tether.

He was not the only one. This was not a rapid change of mind; it accorded with Mussolini's character. He wanted, among other things, to make his Italy an empire, at least like other empires, to make it a military and naval power of top rank. In 1935, he decided to invade and conquer Abyssinia (also as revenge for that savage country's defeat of Italy in 1896). His army accomplished this in less than a year. Now Italy had something like an empire in Africa. The Western Powers did little more than approve entirely useless economic sanctions against Italy. Italy renounced its membership in the League of Nations; so, too, had Germany and Japan. Then the Spanish Civil War started, in July 1936. "Spain's clocks run differently from Europe's other clocks": this adage was often repeated, not without reason. In 1931, the Spanish elections put an end to the more than one-thousand-year-old Spanish monarchy and installed a parliamentary republic, leaning more and more to the Left. Mussolini said this was a retrograde move to a decrepit situation that had existed more than a century before. He was not altogether wrong. In the early Thirties, there were sufficient episodes of anarchy and chaos in Spain to spawn a reaction. A large part of the Spanish army revolted in July 1936, but it could not topple the republic in more than half of Spain. So—in contrast to other events in Spanish history—this was not a coup d'état, but a civil war. It lasted until March 1939, ending with the victory of the right-wing forces (which included many Fascists and sympathizers) and a new state, under the dictatorship of General Francisco Franco. His forces had the support of arms and even troops from Mussolini's Italy and aviators from Hitler's Germany—another considerable change on the political map of Europe before the Second World War.

But by the spring of 1939, there were many others, even more important ones. Early in 1938, Hitler decided to—finally—annex Austria to his Germany. (Before that, he achieved his domination over the leadership of the German army, dismissing conservative generals in favor of unhesitatingly loyal ones.) On February 12, 1938, the Austrian chancellor, Kurt Schuschnigg (Dollfuss's successor), traveled to Berchtesgaden to meet with Hitler, where the latter bullied and threatened him, forcing him to include a leading Austrian National Socialist in the Vienna government. After that, the desperate Austrian chose to set up a plebiscite, the careful terms of which would somehow affirm the independence of Austria. Two days before the plebiscite, Hitler ordered German regiments to march into Austria. Schuschnigg was arrested. Two days later, Hitler himself drove into his native country, stopping at his birthplace and then in Linz, a town very dear to him.

He was overwhelmed by the jubilation of enormous crowds. Then and there, he decided to go further than the establishment of a National Socialist Austria, dependent on Germany. He proclaimed its annexation, the union of Germany and Austria. Then he went on to Vienna, where he faced—if that is the proper word—an even larger ocean of enthusiasts (including the Catholic cardinal of Austria, who stretched out his arm in a Nazi salute, for which he was later chastised by the Vatican, but that did not much matter). The British and French governments did nothing.

Immediately after Austria, Hitler turned on Czechoslovakia.

That was different. The Czechs had a military and political alliance with France, and even one with Soviet Russia. There were almost three million Germans, the so-called Sudetens, living within the natural borders of the Czech state. Hitler's argument rested on the principle of national self-determination (another of Woodrow Wilson's disastrous doctrines). German people within Central Europe belonged to Germany. Not all of the Sudetens were National Socialists, but most of them now were. Unless they were to join Germany, Hitler threatened war. The British government attempted to mediate, but with no result. The French now considered war, and—again reluctantly—so did their British allies. (The Soviet Union did nothing.) At the very last moment, British premier Neville Chamberlain got a message from Hitler inviting him and the French prime minister, Edouard Daladier, to fly to Munich for a conference. Chamberlain—and many, many other people—were instantly relieved. There would be no European war. Chamberlain and Daladier (and Mussolini, who also was invited), agreed to everything Hitler wanted. That big mountain semicircle of Czechoslovakia and its three million inhabitants were given to Hitler. At the end of the conference, Chamberlain and Hitler even signed a declaration in favor of German-British friendship. On his return to London, Chamberlain waved that paper and said: "Peace with honour. I believe it is peace in our time."

Czecho-Slovakia (the very spelling of the name changed) was now in the German sphere, a near-satellite of Hitler. Yet Hitler did not believe in a lasting peace. He was worried about British political leaders and British public opinion critical of him. He was also beginning to turn against Poland, the reduction of whose independence was his next object, together with a cession of western Polish regions and Danzig, still inhabited by a fair number of Germans. He had already started preparations against Poland when another chance arose for him, which he took—for once, mistakenly so. The Slovak nationalists—in cahoots with Hitler—wanted to break up the remnant Czecho-Slovak state. Hitler agreed; and then he decided to occupy and put an end to the rest of Czechia (mostly Bohemia and Moravia). He and his troops marched into Prague on March 15, 1939. One week later, he forced Lithuania to surrender the region of Memel, another slice of Eastern Europe, formerly part of a German empire, with some German population.

These events brought about a revolution in British foreign policy—indeed, in Britain's destiny thereafter. Until then (and here and there, even thereafter), Chamberlain and his minions had not abandoned the hope that they could reach some kind of agreement with Hitler. There were two main reasons for this. One of them was obvious: it was the dread of another world war, only twenty-one years after the end of the First, the world war in which more than one million British and Empire soldiers had died. The other was more complex and less reasonable. It had much to do with the tiredness and shortsightedness of many of the British people in the Thirties; but even more important was Chamberlain's preference (and he was not alone in this) for Hitler and Germany over Communism (though let me add: without much sympathy for National Socialism as such). All of this changed within a week. Hitler had now broken his promise in Munich. There, he had declared that this was his last territorial demand in Europe. Even more telling was that he had gone beyond his trumpeted wish—his claim that all he wanted was to bring German people into his Reich. But the Czechs were not Germans. Even Chamberlain's government recognized that Hitler was not inclined to stop. Consequently, London decided that a way to deter Hitler was to give a guarantee, meaning an alliance, to Poland: Hitler would know that military action against Poland, unlike the events of Austria and Czechoslovakia, would mean war with Britain and France. In all of Britain's history, this was its first committing alliance with an Eastern European state.

The British and the French now thought the time had come to reach some kind of an alliance with the Soviet Union. After all, Hitler's entire public ideology had proclaimed, almost ceaselessly, his hatred of Communism. Before 1939, the Western Allies were reluctant to seek any concerted policy with Soviet Russia (the latter had been excluded from Munich, despite its military alliance with Czechoslovakia). But by 1939, it was Stalin who was unwilling to commit himself to an alliance with Britain and France. There were small signs of this early enough, the most telling one being his ditching of his commissar for foreign affairs, Litvinov (a Jew), in early May, and his replacement of him with the frozen-faced Vyacheslav Molotov. During the summer of 1939, British and French delegations traveled to Moscow; but their negotiations with Stalin (and Molotov) led nowhere. On the contrary: by late July, there were indications that Moscow was not interested in seeking an alliance with Britain. This accorded perfectly with Hitler's view of the world. He and Stalin exchanged letters. By August 20, the texts of a Soviet-German Nonaggression Treaty were ready. The German foreign minister, Joachim von Ribbentrop, flew to Moscow. The signing ceremony was accompanied by unusual friendly gestures from the Soviet side, including smiles and amiable words from Stalin.

Less than another month later, the Germans and Soviets would divide Poland and also more of Eastern Europe among themselves. For the first time in twenty years, Russia had returned as a principal—perhaps *the* principal—factor in the evolving history of Europe. Their pact in August 1939 was a global political earthquake. It is to the credit of the British and the French that they were not now inclined to change or reverse their commitments to Poland. There were a few useless last attempts to avoid a war; these did not impress Hitler. On the first of September, declaring the pretext of Polish provocations, he sent the German army, navy, and air force to attack Poland. On the third of September—the delay suggested vacillation—Chamberlain's government and then France declared war on Germany.

Thus the second European war, fast developing into a world war, had begun. It had worldwide origins well before its beginning. On the other side of the globe, Japan had begun to grow into a vast empire; and that empire was preparing for a possible war with the United States. In more than one way, some Japanese leaders, especially those of the army, were now emulating the new Germany. (In a way, so was Mussolini, who invaded and annexed Albania to his new Italian empire in April 1939, partly to show that he, too, could do something like Hitler.) By September 1939, the Japanese had occupied almost all of the Chinese ports along the China Sea (and forced the British to give up one of their enclaves). In 1936, some of the Japanese junior officers assassinated government officials whom they saw as their enemies (this was the Japanese version of Germany's Night of the Long Knives in 1934—or rather, the Nazi murder of Dollfuss in the same year). The assassins were tried and executed, but the power of the Japanese army leaders was hardly diminished. In early 1939, a portion of their army was moved to the largely uninhabited westernmost portions of China, where they fought an unpublicized battle with a Soviet army that succeeded in pushing them back into China, a large frontier war involving many hundreds of thousands of troops.

By that time, the division of China into three forces was taking place. There were Chinese Nationalists under Chiang Kai-shek, who made Chungking his capital city; there were the Chinese Communists under Mao Tse-tung, milling about somewhere in the northwestern portions of China; and in Nanking there was now Wang Ching-wei, who was something of a Japanese puppet, yet who believed that China's present and future depended on its close association with Japan. The Japanese navy was more conservative than the Japanese army; indeed, their leaders and strategic visions could on occasion conflict with each other. Ever since the Twenties, both the Japanese and the American navies were considering the prospect of an eventual Japanese-American naval war in the Pacific. Japan had embarked on a very large naval building program. So had the Americans; but when the Second World War broke out, the Japanese naval force in the Pacific was slightly larger than the American one. Admiral Isoroku Yamamoto became chief of the combined Japanese fleet on September 1, 1939 (another of those coincidences that statisticians hate but some historians love). Yamamoto saw the army leaders, with their vision of the world, as both stupid and repellent. He was not in favor of the pending Japanese alliance with Germany and Italy. That would come soon—but not quite yet.

And now, having reached the outbreak of the Second World War, I am compelled to state a qualification to the main thesis with which I began this chapter. Yes, the 1930s were Adolf Hitler's decade. But then, they were also Franklin Roosevelt's. Roosevelt was inaugurated president in early March 1933, almost on the same day that Hitler got his all-empowering vote in the Reichstag. Twelve years later, they died, eighteen days apart, just before the end of the Second World War. They could not have been more different—in their characters, their temperaments, their personalities, their views of their tasks and of the world at large. Yes, Hitler put an end to the Depression in Germany very soon; some of America's Depression lasted, by and large, until 1939— but Roosevelt's achievement proved to be more enduring. During that same decade, he won the support of sizable American majorities. He was building up a large American navy. In the eyes of almost all of the world, the reputation and prestige of the United States in 1939 were not only uncompromised, but perhaps higher than ever. At the same time, Roosevelt abhorred Hitler. He was reluctant—or perhaps not ready—to commit himself and the United States to entering another European war; but by 1939, it was more than evident that he was willing to be a main adversary of Hitler in more than one way. The Thirties were his decade; and much of the future would be his, as well.

But before we get there, we must move on to the first two years of the Second World War—and consider that had it been not Roosevelt but someone like Herbert Hoover who had been president of the United States in 1940, Hitler would have won the war.

10

"I HOPE IT IS NOT TOO LATE"

The Second World War—The European phase, 1939 to 1941
—Germany triumphant—Five leaders

THE RELUCTANCE OF BRITAIN and France to go to war was followed by a largely reluctant war ("the phony war," in American parlance: a few small skirmishes along the French-German frontier). Not reluctant was Hitler's Germany—except that his air force did not bomb France or Britain until May 1940. There were no such restraints in the German war against Poland—brutal, destructive, swift as that was. Before the end of September 1939, Warsaw fell and the brave and resolute Polish army had ceased to exist (except for portions of it that struggled to reach France and especially Britain, where their military contribution to the Allies turned out to be highly remarkable throughout the entire war). Even before the end of the Polish war, a fatal stab in Poland's back was administered not by Hitler, but by Stalin. On September 17, his Soviet Union invaded eastern Poland. That was part and parcel of the Russian-German division of much of Eastern Europe, signed in Moscow ten days later. The eastern half of prewar Poland—plus the Baltic republics of Lithuania, Latvia, and Estonia, along with Finland and a section of northern Romania—Hitler allotted to the Russian sphere of interest (whatever that could mean).

One result of this was more proof of the unpredictability of history. Less than three months after the British and French declared war against Germany, the only fighting in Europe was between Russia and Finland. The Russian-German treaty was not precise about what "sphere of interest" meant. Not precise, but rather obvious. Finland was an exception. Its government refused to accept Russia's demands, knowing what they meant. So, by the end of November 1939, the Soviet Union bombed and invaded Finland. The Finns fought back, and very well indeed. Soon, the world saw a war between David and Goliath. In more than one frozen meadow or snow-laden forest of battle, a Russian army had to retreat. Soon, international repercussions arose. Both the British and the French believed that here was a chance for them to break out of the reluctant war and open up a front in the north of Europe, establishing their presence in northern Scandinavia, helping the Finns, scoring some kind of triumph against Hitler's new allies the Russians. Britain and France had already made some preparations when Hitler struck against them. He mediated a quick peace between Finland and Russia whereby Finland lost some territory but kept most of its integrity, without becoming part of Stalin's empire.

It was a political-diplomatic victory for Hitler, who now decided that he ought to go further and chase the British, on land and at sea, out of Scandinavia for good. There would be no northern front against Germany. He largely succeeded. The fact that the British fleet was stronger than the German made little difference. On April 9, 1940, the German army invaded and occupied Denmark within a few hours. Norway was more difficult, since the Norwegian army and its king fought on. But save for the far-northern bay and port of Narvik, German sailors and soldiers occupied just about all of the Norwegian ports before the British. Despite the ruggedness of that northern terrain, the Germans controlled all of Norway in hardly more than a month. The king had to flee to Britain. Sweden remained alone (though its government thought it best to make a few concessions to Hitler).

As a result, the premiership of Neville Chamberlain came to an end. After a hard debate in the House of Commons (where even a large number of his Conservatives abandoned him), he still tried to stay in power, but on May 10, 1940, he had to resign. It was—or at least seemed—obvious that all through the previous weeks and months and years, his determined adversary Churchill had been right. Now King George VI had to invite Churchill to Buckingham Palace, to entrust him with forming a new government. Late in the afternoon on May 10, Churchill left the palace. In the car, he was alone with Inspector W. H. Thompson, his customary bodyguard, who congratulated Churchill: "I only wish the position had come your way in better times, for you have an enormous task." Churchill, unlike Hitler, was a man of unrepressed feelings. Tears, on some occasions, would come into his eyes. This was one of them. He said to Thompson, "God alone knows how great it is. I hope it is not too late. I am very much afraid it is. We can only do our best."

It looked as if it were too late. The speed and talents of the German army were nightmarish. In four days they conquered Holland. In eight days they were in Brussels, and the king of Belgium was contemplating his surrender. In less than four days they had swept away the Ninth French Army, and by May 16 there was alarmingly little between them and Paris. But the strategy employed by the German army (and Hitler) was different from that used in past German invasions of France. The German forces headed not for Paris (yet), but for the Channel coast. They reached it four days later. There were now almost 300,000 British troops in France, cut off from the rest of France by the German army (and from England by the Channel). By the twenty-fourth of May, the Germans had taken every one of the ports of northwestern France except for the northernmost one, Dunkirk. Hitler ordered them to halt there for two days, a decision to which I will return.

Now came a most serious crisis in the most secret conclave of the government of Britain, the nearly full records of which were not available until 1971, when the government opened them. Churchill himself chose not to refer to it when wrote his *History of the Second World War.* It involved the so-called War Cabinet of five men: Churchill, Chamberlain (still head of the Conservative Party), Viscount Halifax (still foreign secretary), and Clement Attlee and Arthur Greenwood, two representatives of the minority of the Labour Party who were now part of the national government. By late on May 16, a Sunday, they knew, more or less, that France would be defeated, that Britain might have to face the prospect of fighting a world war alone. Halifax now chose to confront Churchill. He believed, not without reason, that it was not in Hitler's interest to destroy Britain and its empire entirely; that (with some kind of mediation through Mussolini) British leadership should at least ascertain what kind of terms Hitler might offer. Halifax was appalled by what he saw as Churchill's shortsighted impetuosity. He was not a sympathizer of Hitler or of National Socialism. He was a cool, pragmatic Englishman and had behind him the mass of the Conservative Party, who still distrusted Churchill.

For five most crucial days, Churchill said no. If the British

now approached Hitler, Churchill believed, they would be step-
ping on a slippery slope. "Slippery slope": that was the sum total
of his argument. On the afternoon of May 28, a Thursday, he left
the War Cabinet and spoke to twenty-five men of his Outer Cabinet and a few other politicians. "Of course, whatever happens at
Dunkirk, we shall fight on." He received an encouraging acco-
lade. Within the War Cabinet, it was also to his decisive advantage that Chamberlain did not oppose him by siding with Halifax. One or two days later, Churchill's debate with Halifax was
over. Churchill had won.

By that time—the thirtieth of May—the news from Dunkirk
was better, too. With the indispensable help of a motley array of
British ships, nearly all of the encircled British army, and almost
100,000 French soldiers as well, were evacuated safely to England: a brave endeavor, that was (though with relatively little interference from the Germans, except for their severe bombing of
the beaches and quays). We do not know—and probably will
never know—why Hitler refrained from annihilating or captur-
ing the British army at Dunkirk. There are two possible explana-
tions—especially for his May 24 "halt order" (which was sent to
the army chiefs "in clear"—that is, uncoded—and was consequently heard by the British, though we cannot be sure this was
Hitler's intention). There is some evidence that Hitler thought
his army, especially his armored divisions, needed some rest after fourteen days of advances, and he was not inclined to risk
outrunning his luck. There is even more evidence, from some of
his private comments, that he did not wish to destroy all of the
British; that he thought the latter were or would soon be inclined
to consider a peace proposal; and that the very existence of a nation depended on not losing its army. (He repeated this for the

last time in 1945, when he spoke of his having allowed the British a "golden bridge" in 1940, which was of course an exaggeration.)

What Hitler did not yet know was the kind of man he was up against. Churchill's speeches, his patriotic and historical rhetoric in June 1940, had a perhaps astonishing—in any event profound—effect on his nation. A month later, most of the Conservatives' distrust of Churchill had begun to melt away. There was yet another arrow in Churchill's quiver, or call it a potential ace to play. As early as May 15, he had written a most serious letter to Roosevelt—suggesting, among other things, that without the support of the United States, Britain might not be able to hold out alone. He knew that the American president would respond to this, though he did not yet know how; but he also knew that in Roosevelt's view, Hitler and his power were a deadly danger to Western civilization. It took some time for Hitler to recognize what the United States would do. Meanwhile, he was the ruler of most of Europe—of an even larger area than Napoleon had conquered.

On June 14, the German army was in Paris. Two days later, Churchill offered a complete British-French Union, including joint citizenship. There was no French response. Indeed, the wartime French government had fallen. A new French regime, under the aged Marshal Philippe Pétain, assumed power. Pétain not only disliked the British; he believed that combat against Germany must end and that a new France must accommodate itself to Hitler's Germany, in more than one way. A few days later, he signed an armistice with Germany. Hitler's terms were harsh but not impossible. He did not occupy all of France; he left a more or less sovereign state, an unoccupied zone under Pétain, amounting to about 40 percent of prewar France (of course, none of its coast opposite England); he did not demand that France hand over its colonies, or its impressive navy, though its ships were forced to stay under German supervision. Many of the superb French battleships went to be anchored in the French North African port of Mers-el-Kébir, or Oran, where on July 2 the British gave them an ultimatum: sail to a British port or to American ports in the Caribbean, or they would be attacked. The French admiral rejected this. Immediately, the British navy attacked and sank some of them. Churchill, forever Francophile, ordered this with a heavy heart. Still, it did him nothing but good. Roosevelt and the Americans were much impressed. So was the British Conservative party. Now Hitler ordered the first preparations for an eventual invasion of England.

On June 10, Mussolini's Italy declared war on France and Britain. A few days later, Stalin decided to incorporate the unfortunate Baltic states into the Soviet Union, plus the slice of Romania that had been allotted to him. The Japanese army, too, chose to take advantage of the collapse of the French and Dutch Southeast Asian empires: it moved into northeast French Indochina and began preparing for the control of Dutch Indonesia. This was not all. Throughout the states that his Germany occupied, Hitler found enough people to do his bidding. (The only exception was Poland.) He formally recognized pro-German regimes in each of them. Some of them now had the support of much of their populations, at least in 1940.

Two exceptions were the remaining great powers, America and Russia. From Washington, Franklin Roosevelt was about to organize U.S. support on behalf of Britain, materially and militarily. He knew he had to move against considerable congressional opposition, especially in 1940, when he was preparing to be elected president for the third time, contrary to the American political tradition. He planned for a national cabinet, and he invited two prominent Republicans, Henry Stimson and Frank Knox, to become his secretaries of defense and of the navy. In early August, he decided that it was within his power to transfer fifty old American destroyers to Britain. They arrived there three months later, and had no effect on naval warfare in the Atlantic. Never mind: they represented a symbolic American move of importance. By that time, the correspondence between Churchill and Roosevelt had become voluminous and substantial.

But Hitler was still undecided about his next step—somewhat. Crossing the Channel was not like the crossing of a river, he said. As in the case of Dunkirk, he used air power (which Goering had advised); the sustained bombing of Britain and its cities began in early September. The British people and their government were resolute. Two weeks later, Hitler canceled Operation Sea Lion, the invasion of England. But there was another reason for this change of plans, beyond his growing recognition that you cannot subdue a nation by air power alone: turning his attention eastward, he had ordered initial plans for an eventual invasion of the Soviet Union.

There was method in this kind of madness—if madness it was. Against America, Hitler could do nothing. But if Russia were eliminated, what could Churchill (and Roosevelt) do? Here we must correct a still-popular belief that Hitler was obsessed with Communism. From the outset, he was a committed anti-Communist. Crushing Russia meant the crushing of Communism, and that was potentially agreeable to many anti-Communists throughout the world. This was one element in his calculation, but there was a more important one. It was Britain. As long as Russia existed, Britain had hope. Stalin knew something of that too. Once, after the collapse of France, Churchill had written Stalin a letter, which Stalin had refused to answer or even acknowledge. By then, he was very impressed with Hitler. He wanted to avoid giving Hitler the slightest reason to distrust him; he wished to impress his fellow dictator with his enduring friendship.

But there was still a full year from the capitulation of France to Hitler's invasion of the Soviet Union (June 22, 1940, to June 22, 1941). It was a mixed bag—but, on balance, not a bad year for Hitler. In April 1941, he conquered Yugoslavia and Greece. The latter had been brutally and inexcusably attacked by Mussolini in October 1940. The small Greek army defeated the Italians; one result of this was an expectable alliance of Greece with Britain. Yugoslavia, inspiringly, refused to accept German pressure to join the German alliance system. Two weeks later, Hitler attacked Yugoslavia and broke it up. Another month later, he defeated and expelled the British from Greece and later from Crete, despite the presence of British naval forces around that large island. He now planned to intrude into the Near East, but without much enthusiasm; his great campaign against Russia was soon to begin.

Meanwhile, even before the end of 1940, the British defeated the Italian armies near Egypt (and later in Abyssinia); they also scored impressive victories against the Italian navy. But then, a superb German general, Erwin Rommel, was sent to succor the Axis Powers in north Africa—and so he did, sweeping the British back into Egypt in March and April. Churchill had decided to withdraw a fair number of British troops from Libya in order to sustain the Greeks; but that did not help. Whenever British forces fought Italians, they won; whenever they faced Germans, they almost never did. In early May, another serious bombing of

London began; but soon that diminished because so much of the German air force was to be needed in Russia.

There was one great help for the British throughout these dreary months. It was the increasing support they got from the United States, which was also girding for war, even as Roosevelt thought it best not to proclaim it just yet. A fair number of isolationist laws, passed by Congress before 1939, were eliminated or reduced. The United States moved ahead in the Atlantic, occupying Greenland and Iceland. Elsewhere in the great Atlantic Ocean, American warships made their presence more and more obvious. Hitler ordered the German navy to avoid any response to American provocations, when and where possible. His closest associate, Goebbels, even declared something like a German Monroe Doctrine. It did not resound. On May 10, 1941, Hitler's deputy and very close friend, Rudolf Hess, took it upon himself to fly to England without Hitler's knowledge, in a desperate attempt to make the war between Germany and England cease. Churchill put him in the Tower of London, probably the last famous prisoner there in England's long history. A fortnight later, there was a moment of bright news for the British: their fleet sank the greatest and strongest battleship in the Atlantic, Germany's *Bismarck*.

But soon Churchill was no longer the protagonist in the Second World War. Now there were Hitler and Stalin. The former was determined to attack Russia, and soon. The latter was determined to dissuade him in every possible way. To list Stalin's various, almost endless attempts does not belong in this short history of a century, even though they are revealing. Among other things, they show how and why a crafty, cunning, brutal, capable, realistic, and powerful man can—and will—deceive himself. Stalin did not, perhaps he could not, imagine that Hitler, who was still in the middle of a great Atlantic war with Britain and almost with the United States, would start a second war with Russia. The steps he took to impress Hitler are astonishing in retrospect; in more than one instance, they were less crafty than piteous. Stalin ordered his army not to respond to any German provocation or intrusion along Russia's borders, nor to attack any German aircraft making reconnaissance flights over the western Soviet Union. His minion Molotov said to the German ambassador, hours after the German invasion had begun: "Surely we did not deserve this." (The Soviet ambassador in Berlin: "Are you sure this is not a mistake?")

In April 1941, Stalin made one statesmanlike move from which he would benefit. He offered Japan a nonaggression treaty, which the Japanese government eagerly accepted. Thus, even in the event of a war with Germany, Russia would not have to fight a two-front war. That was a great advantage for Russia, though not for the United States. The Japanese were preparing for an eventual war with America and Britain, but not with the Soviet Union. After the German invasion of the latter, there were some Japanese leaders who proposed to discard their treaty with Russia and attack it instantly in eastern Siberia; but that did not happen.

On June 22, the day of the German invasion, Stalin was profoundly depressed. He could not face speaking to the Soviet people. He told Molotov to do that. In a few days, it appeared that the German armies were cutting through the western Soviet Union with their accustomed ease. On the twenty-eighth, Stalin collapsed. He mumbled a few words suggesting everything was lost. He took refuge in his cottage outside Moscow. Two days later, a Politburo delegation arrived to see him. He thought, at first, that they had come to arrest him. Instead, they told him that he had to lead the Soviet Union; there was no one else. They were probably right. He then pulled himself together and drove back to Moscow. On July 2, he addressed the peoples of the Soviet Union in patriotic tones (which had nothing to do with Communism).

By that time, Italy, Romania, Hungary, Finland, and volunteer forces from other European nations had declared war on the Soviet Union. The German armies surged ahead in Belorussia, the Ukraine, and Russia, at a pace even beyond their accustomed impressive speed. By the end of summer, they had gathered almost two million Soviet prisoners (most of them were put into prison camps in Germany, treated with definite neglect and cruelty, and given very little food, some of the Nazi leaders hoping that this would at least decimate them). There were only a few instances where the resistance of Russian garrisons was considerable.

As early as September 3, Stalin sent a message to Churchill: "The Soviet Union is in mortal peril." The British ought to invade France or the Balkans, and send to Russia "a minimum monthly aid of 400 airplanes and 500 tanks." Ten days later, Stalin asked Churchill to send twenty-five or thirty British divisions to Russia through Archangel or Persia. (Much of the latter, British and Russian forces had occupied without trouble the month before.) Churchill told him that this was impossible. The Germans had conquered Kiev; they surrounded Leningrad (St. Petersburg), where they thought it better to starve out the population and its garrison instead of fighting them from concrete building to concrete building. By the middle of November, the outer group of the German army was getting close to Moscow.

There, they halted for a while. The customary Russian winter, full of mud and snow, contributed much to this; yet in 1941, the weather was somewhat milder than usual. Then, the last push for Moscow (Operation Typhoon) was halted by the Soviet army, now fortified by divisions hauled from the Far East (and also by the first trickle of American and British arms arriving in Russia). Here and there, the Russians began to force the Germans back somewhat; they recaptured the south Russian city of Rostov—a German retreat that was something like a first in the military history of the Second World War.

Hitler was aware of what this meant. Throughout the summer, he kept telling his generals: "When Russia is defeated, this will force England to make peace." Or: "The ultimate objective of the Reich is the defeat of Great Britain." And: "The fall of Moscow might even force England to make peace at once." Significant, too, is what he said on November 19 to General Franz Halder in his headquarters: "The recognition, by both of the opposing coalitions, that they cannot annihilate each other will lead to a negotiated peace." And four days later, Halder recorded another of Hitler's remarks in his war diary: "We must face the possibility that neither of the principal opponents (Germany and Britain) will succeed in annihilating or decisively defeating the other." Note that Hitler spoke thus when the German central front was still inching forward to Moscow—more than two weeks before the Russian counteroffensive at Moscow would begin.

And now Hitler's entire strategy changed. He knew that he could no longer win *his* war—his war of short wars. But he also knew that he still had not lost it—that he could eventually force one or another of his enemies to negotiate an armistice or peace with him.

Before that, he made another decision that affected not the Second World War, but his historical reputation more than seventy years later and probably for a very long time. There was always some difference between his Judeophobia and his early recognition that anti-Semitism could be, and indeed was, a powerful populist and popular asset. But that was not the issue now. Until August or September 1941, his principal purpose regarding the Jews was to eliminate their presence from Germanic Europe through expulsion, forcing and allowing their emigration. Since the beginning of the war in 1939, this had become less and less possible, though some Jewish emigration from Europe, mostly to the Americas, went on. But now he had in his possession large portions of eastern Poland and the Soviet Union, where a great many Jews still lived—more than two million of them. There was no place to expel them. Worse: if Germany were to lose the war, these masses of Jews would be the principal enemies of the German people. So his and his regime's policy changed from expulsion to extermination. Soon, the first gas chambers would be built in Poland. Soon, that policy would be extended to almost every European nation controlled by Germany. The end result, by 1945, was the mass killing of at least five million Jews, as well as political dissidents, ethnic Poles, prisoners of war, mentally impaired individuals, and others.

Meanwhile, Japan and the United States were edging closer to war. In 1940, a new Japanese government that was supported by the army joined a Tripartite Pact—an alliance with Germany and Italy. The commander-in-chief of the Japanese navy, Admiral Yamamoto, who was opposed to the alliance, now had to prepare for a war against the United States. Nor was the Japanese emperor, Hirohito, altogether in favor of such a war. More than a year passed before the attack on Pearl Harbor. Well before that, President Roosevelt and his military leaders made a decision that may have been a most decisive one in the Second World War. The original draftsman of that decision, an unsung hero, was an otherwise quiet and self-effacing admiral, Harold Stark, chief of naval operations at the time. As early as November 1940 he wrote a crucial memorandum, according to which the American navy was not yet strong enough to fight a war in both the Atlantic and the Pacific; and stating that—most important—a war in the Atlantic sustaining Britain and against Germany should be the priority of the United States. This was not yet quite in accord either with popular American sentiment or with the supreme command of the navy; but President Roosevelt agreed instantly, and so did the leaders of the navy and the army. At first called Stark's "Plan D," by early January 1941 it became "Plan ABC" and, later, "Rainbow 5." It involved a drastic revision of the long-standing American war plan ("Orange") that had been in effect for twenty years, contemplating war in the Pacific against Japan. It meant a new two-war strategy, with a redistribution of much of the navy and with Germany (and Europe) being the ultimate concern. And so this became the main purpose and strategy of the United States for the Second World War—indeed, its chosen destiny for the rest of the twentieth century.

Enemies of Roosevelt would call these preliminaries to Pearl Harbor Roosevelt's "Back Door to War." That was a half-truth. What is true is that throughout 1941, Roosevelt tried everything —well, almost everything—to provoke a serious German attack on American warships in the Atlantic, an attack that could serve as a plausible reason (or pretext) for an American declaration of war against Germany. This did not come about. Churchill sailed across the Atlantic in August, his first personal meeting with Roosevelt since 1918, when the latter had been assistant secretary of the American navy (Churchill hardly remembered that encounter, though Roosevelt did). They agreed on many things, including their joint aims, set out in the "Atlantic Charter." Theirs was now a virtual alliance. Still Roosevelt was not yet ready to declare war. More important, for him, was increasing the American military pressure on Japan. During American and Japanese negotiations (which included discussions with Japanese envoys sent to Washington), it appeared, at the latest by November 26, that the newest American demands were for Japan to abandon most, perhaps all, of its recent imperial conquests of China. This the Japanese could not accept. A big task force of the Japanese navy weighed anchor and started eastward for its coming attack on Pearl Harbor. For such a daring surprise attack, the entire American navy in the Pacific and its command in Hawaii were unprepared. As were, of course, the American people.

So the Second World War began, almost *in toto,* on December 7, 1941. It was the end of the still largely European war. It was also a turning point of the entire war. The Russians were stopping the Germans, beginning to push them back somewhat, at the very same time that the United States declared war on Japan, and Germany on the United States, a few days later. I am inclined to draw on Churchill's own account of his evening of December 7, a Sunday. He was tired and in a glum mood. He knew that the Japanese were about to enter the war. But what if, among other things, they attacked and invaded Britain's possessions in the Far East, instead of attacking the Americans? He spoke little; his head was down. Then his butler came in with a piece of news: the Japanese had attacked the United States. Churchill rose instantly and ordered that a phone call be put through to Roosevelt, who confirmed the news.

"No American will think it wrong of me if I proclaim that to have the United States at our side was to me the greatest joy. . . .

So we had won after all! After seventeen months of lonely fighting . . . we had won the war. England would live; Britain would live; the Commonwealth of Nations and the Empire would live. How long the war would last or in what fashion it would end, no man could tell, nor did I, at this moment, care. . . . Hitler's fate was sealed. Mussolini's fate was sealed. As for the Japanese, they would be ground to powder." So it would happen—though it would still take a long time.

This short history of the twentieth century is not a philosophical treatise. But at this point I am compelled to add two brief digressions. The first is a summary of my view of history, which goes contrary to the still very widely accepted categorical beliefs of why and how history happened and happens, of course including that of the Second World War. The current, often deemed "scientific" belief is that history, perhaps especially in the democratic age, is the result of great material and economic factors, of which the lives, acts, and thoughts of people are largely the consequences. That is less than a half-truth. In 1933, Hitler came to power in Germany not just because of the economic crisis of 1930–1933, but because of the political mood of many Germans at that time. It was not the state of the British economy that made the British government reluctant to resist Hitler in the Thirties. It was not inferiority of materials or armaments that led to the collapse of France in 1940. There was no economic reason for the Japanese to plan and then make war on the United States. Of course, it is true that the tremendous material power of the United States (and the enormous size of the armies of the Soviet Union) made the war winnable against Germany and Japan. But there, too, what mattered was the resolution and the near-unanimity of the American people, and the unwillingness of the Russian people to oppose Stalin. What people thought (and think), what they believe, what they choose to think, what they prefer to believe—that is the main essence of their lives, of which their material conditions and economic desires are most often the outcomes, and not the other way around.

This brings me to the second, though not unrelated matter, which is the historical importance of national leaders—especially during the Second World War. Entire libraries have been written and published about most of them. Yet their importance was such that I am compelled to record or describe, necessarily briefly, some matters about them that are not usually thought of. Yes, the main participants in the Second World War were states (and nations): Germany, Britain, France, Italy, the Soviet Union, Japan, the United States, and so on. But a Germany without Hitler? A Britain without Churchill? A United States without Roosevelt? Again, we must at least question the still widely prevalent belief according to which men are, at best, instruments of history; they do not make it. Adolf Hitler was a towering figure in the entire history of the twentieth century. We assess men in history by their consequences. No Hitler: no Second World War. No Hitler—no Soviet occupation of the eastern half of Europe, including eastern Germany. No Hitler—no mass murder of five or six million people. And almost three-quarters of a century after his death, there is a significant minority of people, in many nations, who are still partisans of National Socialism, including anti-Semitism, and who avoid mentioning Hitler for politic reasons, but not because they do not admire him. In plain English: Have we yet to come to terms with Hitler?

We must at the same time consider that Hitler and his mind were complex—not just marked by the fearful simplicity that was also there. To detail the complexity remains the task of present and future historians; it does not fit within the limitations of this book. But because it includes the history of the Second World War, I must list some of these complexities. Hitler did not really want a Second World War, especially not with Britain. His fearful simplicity and eventually his undoing was his inclination to hate, and his discovery that propagating hate may be a useful popular asset. There are many proofs of this in his early political speeches. It may even involve a certain duality in his thoughts about Jews: the crystallization of his own Judeophobia in 1919, together with his even more important recognition that anti-Semitism could be, and indeed was, a potentially popular asset. During the Second World War, there was evidence of this. Yes, Hitler changed the German policy from expelling Jews to exterminating them; but he showed no interest when he was presented with records about how this was proceeding. His last public speech, on April 16, 1945, is telling. He emphasized and excoriated "Jewish Bolshevism," when he certainly knew that Stalin was neither pro-Jewish nor a dogmatic Communist; indeed, he had come to admire Stalin. And we have also seen that, as early as November 1941, he knew he could no longer win the war on his terms; after that, he hoped that he might split his opponents, one of whom would then consider making some kind of deal with him. He was a national and military leader who, alas, also had some abilities as a statesman. He sometimes underestimated his opponents, but he did not underestimate himself; and we must not underestimate him, scourge of history and humanity as he was.

Churchill. Surely we assess him by his consequences. He did not win the Second World War in 1945. But he was the one who, in 1940, did not lose it. Whence his historical grandeur. To this we ought to add that his historical insight and foresight were stunning. He foresaw, perhaps before anyone else, what Hitler meant. Later, he understood Hitler better than Hitler understood him. He understood Stalin and Russia better than Roosevelt did. (Well after the war, he also understood that Stalin would not risk a war with the United States.) Unlike Russia in 1941, England in 1940 could have received an offer of peace from Hitler, who wanted Britain to accept his domination of Europe and end its resistance to Germany. Churchill would not consider that for a moment. He knew this would mean that England would become a partner of Germany, if not a "slave state." In 1940, he was alone, the single obstacle to Hitler's winning the Second World War. In 1941, Stalin was not alone. He was about to become Churchill's and Roosevelt's partner. Yet if Hitler had only halted his armies in 1941, Stalin might have been willing to become his junior part-ner—indeed, to turn over to Hitler portions of his empire, if need be, while the rest of Europe went to hell. Hitler knew this. But he thought that his armies could conquer Russia. In 1940, he was not sure that he could conquer England. Churchill, not Sta-lin, was the obstacle to his complete triumph. Because of this, he hated Churchill and then turned to hate the English people with a fury, till the end. He did not hate Stalin; once his invasion of Russia bogged down, he respected him. He even liked him. Such is the irony of history—or rather, the alchemy of human minds.

One thing we may say in favor of Stalin: his ambitions—con-trary to the belief that was widely accepted for decades after the Second World War—had their limits, not because of his modesty, of course, but probably because of his peasant-like realism. In mid-December 1941, Anthony Eden, Churchill's foreign secre-tary, flew to Moscow. At times, some of the windows of the Kremlin rattled with the echoes of German gunfire, hardly more than fifteen miles away. Among more important matters, they talked about Hitler. "His problem," Stalin said, "is that he does not know when to stop." "Does anyone?" Eden said. "I do," said Stalin.

Franklin Roosevelt's greatest asset was his self-confidence. That impressed his people domestically and, often, his conversants abroad. Added to this was his anti-isolationist belief, which accorded with Churchill's: Hitler's Germany was the primary danger. But his perspective on world history was not the same as Churchill's. This we will see later in the Second World War.

I am inclined to add here another great leader, though one whose power was not comparable to that of the four others sketched above. This was Charles de Gaulle, the leader of Free France and a major contributor to France's military and spiritual liberation. I mention only two instances relevant to 1940. One was that Churchill noticed early the extraordinary character of this man during his rapid and inconclusive air journeys to Paris, before the French collapse: one man among the dozens of deeply agitated and vexed French politicians and generals, a two-star general in the background who spoke little. "The Constable of France," Churchill was supposed to have muttered on one occasion. The other matter is that we ought not to exaggerate de Gaulle's numberless conflicts and arguments with Churchill during the war—indeed, exasperating the latter more than once —without keeping in mind de Gaulle's purpose: to demonstrate to the world that he was more than a satellite of the British. Let us note one crucial short sentence in de Gaulle's *Memoirs*. Bereft, he had decided to fly to Britain alone during the collapse of France. He hoped to do something for his country—but what? Then Churchill gave him the chance to broadcast to (and for) France. So, many years later, de Gaulle wrote: "Without him, I could have done nothing."

11

TO SUBDUE AND CONQUER GERMANY AND JAPAN

After Pearl Harbor, six months of Allied defeats—The naval and military turning points of the war—German ability to carry on—Mussolini eliminated—Turning the tide in the east—The Allied invasion of France—Hitler's determination —The conquest of Japan

It took Britain, Russia, and the United States three and a half years to subdue and conquer Germany and Japan. In the case of Germany, one of them—and possibly even any two of them together—could not have accomplished that. In the war against Japan, the enormous power of the United States, together with the resolution of its people, could and did accomplish it.

Immediately after Pearl Harbor, the Western Allies suffered defeat after defeat. Churchill had sent two of the top British battleships to Malaya to impress the Japanese, whose airplanes sank both of them two days after Pearl Harbor. Thereafter, the Japanese army moved swiftly to conquer one British possession in the Far East after another. Most depressing was their occupation of Singapore in February 1942, where they met with a lamentably feeble British defense. By that time, Japan was victorious everywhere. Its navy ventured as far as the Indian Ocean, shelling

Ceylon. It now dominated much of the Pacific. The United States had to surrender some of its mid-Pacific islands to Japan. For a while, it seemed as if the Japanese were moving south toward Australia. They tried to set foot in New Guinea. In May came the first great battle between the Japanese and American navies, the battle of the Coral Sea, which was something of a draw.

Meanwhile the British, after a temporary advance in December, were once again driven back westward by Rommel. In Russia, the Germans were pushed back here and there during the winter. That meant no decisive victory for the Soviet armies. The Germans, so Hitler exulted in April, mastered a winter and a fate that had destroyed Napoleon 130 years before. In June, they started another chapter in their war: an offensive not toward Moscow but toward the south, in the direction of the Caucasus, and after that, presumably, toward the Near East.

Yet even before that came the greatest military (more exactly, naval) turning point of the war. This was the American victory at Midway on June 4–5, 1942. After the Coral Sea, it was the first great sea battle between aircraft carriers, not between battleships. The Japanese air force at Pearl Harbor had sunk or damaged six American battleships, a spectacular achievement, but one without grave consequences in the course of modern naval warfare, since battleships were no longer primary. It was now aircraft carriers that mattered, since the bombers they carried could damage and sink other ships (including the carriers of their enemies) more accurately and effectively than battleships could. The Japanese knew that. Midway was, of course, in the very middle of the Pacific. The Americans had one crucial advantage. This was the ability of their superb code-breakers to decipher and read Japan's secret instructions to its naval force and thereby reveal the locations and movements of the Japanese war fleet approaching Midway. This was crucial, but not necessarily decisive. Decisive was the dauntless bravery, here and there amounting to heroism, of most of the American fliers (together with the steadfast leadership of their admiral, Raymond Spruance). At first, there were painful failures on both sides (for example, the American torpedoes fired by those intrepid fliers did not work). But sometime around noon on June 4, the tide turned: the Americans began to damage and sink three or four Japanese carriers, while losing only one of their own. The great Japanese central navy force moved away. It would never threaten American islands again; and the American rule of much of the Pacific began to expand westward, toward Japan. Still, it took more than two years to subdue Japanese-held islands, one after the other, and also to reconquer the Philippines, which the Japanese had captured earlier in the war.

Had the Japanese won at Midway (and that was very close), Admiral Yamamoto's plan was to end the war against the United States with a treaty advantageous for Japan, as was the case after the Russo-Japanese war in 1904–1905. But would the American government—and the American people—have agreed to that? Yamamoto did not underestimate either the power or the resolution of the American people. It is regrettable that a year after Midway, President Roosevelt—again informed by a decoded Japanese message identifying a single plane carrying Yamamoto over an island in the western Pacific—ordered the American naval air corps to destroy him. The gallant admiral did not deserve his fate; but that was of no consequence for the further development of the war.

There were more disasters coming to the British. Less than two weeks after Midway, on the other side of the world, General Rommel beat 30,000 British and Commonwealth troops into

Tobruk, in northern Libya, and forced them to surrender another ten days later. He now advanced to the western border of Egypt, where the British blocked him, not without difficulties. There was another, greater problem that weighed upon Churchill. This was that of the "Second Front"—and: What to do with Russia? How to deal with Stalin's distrust? The enormous mass of the German army was deep into Russia, but there was yet no British or American plan to open a front in Western Europe to force Hitler to fight a real two-front war. Navies were one thing; the air war against Germany was another. The supplies and armaments sent to Russia by the British and the Americans were yet another. But what did they amount to, compared to the frightful weight of the war bearing down on the Russian armies? Stalin's obsession with a Second Front was more than propaganda. At the same time, an incessant drumbeat on behalf of a Second Front was carried on by Communist and other Leftist sympathizers in Britain and in the United States.

The American Joint Chiefs of Staff *were* actually planning for a Second Front: an invasion of Western France in November 1942. Churchill was convinced that this would be a disaster. So he flew across the Atlantic again to talk to Roosevelt. For almost the last time in the Second World War, he was about to persuade the Americans. They were—reluctantly—accepting the British view that an invasion of France in late 1942 should be postponed to 1943 (eventually it took place, a year and a half later). Then, Roosevelt, who was convinced that in 1942, somewhere and somehow, an American army should confront the Germans, agreed that an American invasion of French North Africa should be mounted, by November of that year. Upon his return to London, Churchill had to face an unprecedented effort to censure his leadership in the House of Commons. It was rejected by a large majority.

But now before him loomed another difficult task. He had to appease Stalin. "I am carrying a lump of ice to the North Pole," Churchill said to his wife. He flew to Moscow in early August. At the beginning—indeed, for a few days and nights—he had to endure and confront Stalin's rude complaints ("Why are the British afraid to fight the Germans?"). On the last night, a few hours before Churchill was to fly back to London from Moscow, there was a change in atmosphere, as well as in substance. There was a personal rapport which suggested that Stalin was as loath to abandon his alliance with the British as the British were to break with him. Churchill told Stalin of the American-British invasion of French North Africa that was to take place within a few months. Stalin instantly comprehended and welcomed the strategic import of that.

Thereafter came multiple turning points in the military history of the Second World War. A new British commander, Bernard Montgomery, decided that his Eighth Army was now strong enough to attack the Germans and drive them out of Egypt into Libya and beyond. That led to his victory at El Alamein in late October. Two weeks later, the Americans landed in French North Africa. Another ten days later, the Sixth German Army, part of the large army group now beginning to move back from the northern Caucasus, was encircled by the Russians and forced to fall back to the city of Stalingrad on the Volga. The Americans had difficulties dislodging the remnant German troops in Tunisia; but meanwhile, Montgomery moved ahead and joined up with the Americans. At the end of January 1943, the Sixth German Army surrendered in Stalingrad. At the end of April, the remnant German (and some Italian) units surrendered in Tunis, whereby the Axis presence in Africa came to an end.

Hitler's Germany fought on, not always without success, for the next two years and more. He himself accepted his responsibility for Stalingrad, so he said. At the same time, Stalingrad was a very large and bloody battle—but considering the human loss, not larger than Verdun in 1916. There was a difference: Verdun was not a turning point of the First World War, but after Stalingrad the Germans had to retreat almost everywhere. Their retreat westward across Russia, and then beyond it, was impressively careful and able. In 1941 and 1942, the Germans took fifteen months to reach Stalingrad from Berlin (and five months to reach the outskirts of Moscow). From 1942 to 1945, the Russians took twice as long to advance from Stalingrad to Berlin (and more than a year to drive the Germans out of Russia altogether). There was even something like a lull over most of the long Russian-German front until the early summer of 1943. It was followed by a last great German offensive at Kursk, with indecisive results. Meanwhile, the Anglo-American aerial bombing of Germany went on incessantly. But it did not decide the war, and there was no invasion of Western Europe in 1943.

It was now evident that the next object of the Anglo-American armies would be Sicily. They invaded it on July 10. The effect on Italy was obvious; it came soon. A fortnight later, the majority of the Grand Council of Fascist Italy voted against Mussolini. Next day, King Victor Emmanuel III called Mussolini to the royal palace and told him to resign. When Mussolini left the palace, an automobile took him to a place of sequestration. That was the sudden end of the Fascist era. Most Italians were jubilant. General Pietro Badoglio was named prime minister. The war continued—but of course, Italy's abandonment of the war was already being discussed by secret Italian and Allied envoys. On September 3, Allied troops crossed from Sicily to Italy. Five days later, the armistice—that is, the surrender of Italy to the Allies—was declared. Hitler and the Germans were ready for this. Instantly, German and SS troops occupied most of Italy's cities, including Rome. The king and the government fled to the south. Most of the Italian navy and much of the army were loyal to the king; soon, much of the navy sailed over to the Allies. Hitler sent a daring glider troop to rescue Mussolini from the mountain house where he had been interned. There were now two Italies— one in the south, the other a shadow government set up in the north, eventually presided over by Mussolini. Italy and its people were ravaged, suffering until almost the very end of the war.

The Allied campaign in Italy was not impressive. By the end of September, the Allied armies had gotten as far as Naples, but hardly beyond. It took them more than eight months to reach Rome, which they did on June 4, 1944, two days before D-Day in France. In some ways, Churchill was responsible for this. Partly because of his knowledge of the British historical tradition, in which naval power often decided a war, and partly because of his no less historical memory of how a war in northern France might be a repetition of the horrible bloodshed there during the First World War, he was anxious about the prospects of an Anglo-American invasion of Western Europe, though he kept this anxiety to himself. Yes, the Mediterranean was the "soft underbelly" of Europe; and the Mediterranean, by the end of 1943, was now an inland sea, largely ruled by the Allied navies—but that did not decide the war. (One statistic: in 1943, Germany produced almost as many airplanes as did the United States—despite the widespread bombing of German factories and cities.)

By the end of 1943, the Russian armies had reached the prewar borders of the Soviet Union in most places. The Allied, especially American, armaments and vehicles sent to Russia had become a flood. Yet the absence of a serious Second Front, and the limitations of British convoys sailing for Russia north of Norway, whence they were often attacked by German airplanes, vexed Stalin. He made that obvious. As late as 1943, Roosevelt and especially Churchill still had to worry about the possibility that Stalin might make a deal with Hitler. That danger faded, especially because Stalin saw that Hitler would be beaten and that eventually his Soviet Union could get more from the Western Allies than he now could from Hitler. Consequently, the table was set for the first Three-Power Summit—for his meeting with Roosevelt and Churchill in Teheran at the end of November 1943. It is telling that, in order to accommodate Stalin, these world leaders were willing to travel across the globe to meet him in or close to Russia (Teheran was then in the Russian occupation zone of Persia— today, Iran).

The Teheran Summit remains significant for more than one reason. Stalin still thought that Churchill did not have his heart set on the coming invasion of France. But his suspicion faded as their meetings went on. At the same time, a considerable topic was that of Turkey. Turkey was a British ally that Stalin disliked. Churchill was still eager to get Turkey into the war and open a Balkan front against the Germans. This did not happen; but it is telling how much of the conference dealt with Europe. Stalin had already broken relations with the legitimate Polish government-in-exile; it was evident that a problem was not so much the future borders of Poland but the character of its postwar regime. A very important feature of the conference was that it provided evidence of the inclinations of Roosevelt. He was less interested in postwar Europe than was Churchill. More important: he moved closer to Stalin ("Uncle Joe") and away from Churchill. He demonstrated this several times in Teheran. He believed that good

American-Russian relations were now more important than his earlier ones with Britain. (One reason for this was his wish to make Stalin join the war against Japan, which Stalin promised to do.) There was a deeper reason—namely, his historical perspective, which was not Churchill's. Roosevelt saw (and this went beyond his view of the war) that the United States was in the middle between Britain and Russia—historically, that is. Britain, as represented by Churchill, was venerable and old. Soviet Russia, as represented by Stalin, was a rough, advancing nation that embodied something crude but new. The United States, democratic and progressive, was historically in the middle between them—so Roosevelt thought. He was wrong. Russia was not ahead of the United States (or of Britain), but well behind.

Hitler was not entirely uninformed of what happened in Teheran, but he could take no solace from that. His army had to face more or less serious guerrilla attacks in Yugoslavia and Greece. The governments of his allies started to have some contacts with the Western Allies. In March 1944 he occupied Hungary, installing an extreme pro-German regime there. The day after Rome fell, British and American armies, transported and supported by a huge armada, landed in Normandy. On July 20, a group of patriotic German officers, together with some high officers including Rommel, attempted to get rid of Hitler and save what they still could for their Germany. That coup d'état was ill-prepared. Hitler himself survived the detonation of a bomb that had been placed in his headquarters. The plotters were executed; later, Rommel was offered a choice between a trial and suicide. On August 21, de Gaulle's Free French soldiers and American troops entered Paris. Before that, another American invasion landed along the Mediterranean shores of France, which were largely undefended by the Germans. Churchill had been against that: he had wanted such an invasion to occur in the Italian Adriatic, where an Allied army could advance into northern Yugoslavia and south-central Europe. He no longer had his way. After D-Day, many more American troops than British were in combat against the Germans. Romania changed its regime and surrendered to Russia in less than twenty-four hours. The Russians had Bulgaria surrender to them; by late September, they had entered Hungary.

Before that ended, one of the most regrettable episodes of the Second World War occurred. By the end of July, the Russian army was close to Warsaw—indeed, some of it stood across that capital city, on the eastern bank of the River Vistula. The Home Army of Poland, civilians and former soldiers, an admirable patriotic force, rose up against the German occupiers of Warsaw. The Home Army kept the latter at bay for almost two months. Of course, the Home Army had a political reason: to liberate Warsaw themselves, to impress the world and the Russians, who would then find it difficult to ignore these brave Poles. But the Russians did. Capable of cynical calculation as they were, they gave the Poles little help or none at all. Stalin himself accused the Poles of "adventurism." He had already installed his own satellite Polish "government" in eastern Poland.

A division of postwar Europe was already taking shape. Churchill was deeply concerned with this. (Roosevelt was not.) So he flew suddenly to Moscow in October. In the very first hour of his meeting with Stalin, he proposed that there should be no conflict between Russia and Britain, or between their spheres of interest in Eastern Europe. He put a paper before Stalin, his "Percentages

Agreement." Russia would have 90 percent influence in Romania and Bulgaria; Britain, 90 percent in Greece; in Yugoslavia and Hungary, the split would be 50–50 (the latter ratio then was amended by Molotov to 80–20 in Russia's favor). Stalin looked at the paper and marked his agreement in an instant. Churchill knew that he had to save Greece, where, after its liberation, a crude civil war was going on between Greek Communists and royalists. In December, he sent a British division to Greece. Then he had to leave his English home at Christmas, and flew to Athens to help construct a proper Greek government. Five weeks later, the Greek Communists were defeated. All through these months, Stalin kept his word. His troops stood on the northern border of Greece, but he gave no help and not a single word of support for the Greek Communists. Across the Atlantic, the British were excoriated as imperialists by much of the American press, and even by some in Britain.

Churchill had saved Greece, but perhaps that was all. At the same time, we must credit him for his foresight. When he visited Paris in November, de Gaulle was critical of the Americans, among other things. De Gaulle said: They are letting the eastern half of Europe go to the Russians. Churchill said that he knew this, but that he could do little or nothing. Russia was now "a hungry wolf in the midst of sheep; but after the meal will come the digestion period." Russia would not be able to digest most of its conquests.

And the war was not yet over. The Allies had freed France and most of Belgium; but they had not penetrated western Germany, nor had they yet crossed the Rhine. Already a fortnight after the fall of Paris, Hitler gave orders to plan for a German counteroffensive in the west. So it came. In December, a German army attacked an American army in eastern Belgium. The Germans advanced nearly fifty miles but they were not able to go farther toward Antwerp, which had been Hitler's aim.

There was a moment of panic, but the Americans recovered fast. This "Battle of the Bulge" may have retarded the Allied advance into Germany proper, but not by much.

In early February, Roosevelt, Stalin, and Churchill met again, at Yalta. There, the American president was something like the principal figure; in spite of his increasing physical weakness, he got two promises from Stalin. Russia would go to war against Japan three months after the surrender of Germany (a promise that Stalin kept, to the day). The other was a goal dear to Roosevelt: the Soviet Union would join the United Nations. The latter was part of the American president's ideal of a postwar international order in which the Soviet Union would actively participate. There were discussions about Poland, without results. There was no serious consideration about the already forming division of Europe that soon became the prime theater of the coming Cold War between America and Russia, beginning less than two years after Yalta.

By March 1945, the American and Russian (and British) armies began to move forward across Germany. The end of the war was in sight, though there was little optimism or even relief. Much of Europe, especially in the center of the continent, was in ruins. Millions of people either had been forced out of their homelands or had chosen, in desperation, to flee. The march of the Russians toward and into Germany was one long sweep of barbarism, replete with rape, robbery, and destruction unprecedented in the history of Europe for many centuries. Here and there, when the fighting ended in early summer, a wan sunshine played over many lunar cityscapes even at noon.

Roosevelt died suddenly, on April 12. Mussolini was murdered by some of his own people seventeen days later. Hitler killed himself on April 30. Till the end, he nurtured some hopes that his enemies would split apart; among other things, he did not discourage the negotiations that happened between Germans (including SS leaders) and Americans in Italy over several months. Among his hierarchs, General Heinrich Himmler began to negotiate with Americans and even with Jews; Goering left Berlin. Goebbels remained there, killing himself and his entire family two days after the Führer, whose last testament to the German people had not much new to say, except that he was aware of the differences between East and West. He appointed Admiral Karl Doenitz (Western-inclined) and Goebbels (Russian-inclined) as his successors.

The American army halted about sixty miles west of Berlin around April 12, allowing the Russians to conquer the capital of Germany. Their last offensive began five days later. The remnant German troops in Berlin surrendered to the Russians on May 2, and the chiefs of the German army, navy, and air force capitulated six days later in Rheims. In Europe, the Second World War was over. It ended with neither a bang nor a whimper.

In the Pacific, the Americans made straight for Japan. In 1943 and 1944, they landed on and then conquered several of the Marianas and Gilbert Island. In October 1944, General Douglas MacArthur landed in the Philippines. A large naval battle occurred in Leyte Gulf, where much of what was left of the Japanese navy was destroyed or damaged. The British began to advance against the Japanese in Burma. In early 1945, a massive American aerial bombing burned down large parts of Tokyo; perhaps as many as 100,000 inhabitants perished there.

The Japanese now depended on two kinds of desperate attempts to slow the American advance. One was the incredible struggle of a few thousands or even fewer of their soldiers, with hardly more than rifles, fighting the Americans moving into their islands. Examples of these were Tarawa, Iwo Jima, Okinawa —the last in April 1945, already close to Japan. The losses on both sides were astonishingly great, though the numbers of the Japanese dead were often eight times those of the Americans. The other strategy was to employ suicide planes (the so-called kamikaze), which hurled themselves onto the decks of American warships with their pilots and crew aboard. Considerable their damages were overall; decisive, not. Still, the American leadership, including the new president, Harry Truman, had to plan for the invasion of Japan in 1946, with the prospect of numerous American casualties.

That dreadful invasion proved unnecessary. Even before the atomic bombings of Hiroshima and Nagasaki, Emperor Hirohito and other devoted Japanese leaders wanted to end the war, no matter how. Already the Japanese government was transformed, now led by conservatives and moderates. They kept asking Moscow to mediate between Tokyo and Washington, but in vain. In July 1945, the Potsdam Summit (the last in the war, with Stalin, Churchill, and Truman) had still insisted on the doctrine of unconditional surrender; but prudently, the president and his advisers no longer mentioned the condition that the Japanese emperor must be removed. In early August, there were many signals suggesting a Japanese wish to surrender, now through the diplomatic intermediary of Switzerland. On August 10, the Japanese government's decision was made; it was communicated to the world.

A few days before, two tremendous disasters had befallen Japan. One was the Americans' dropping of two atomic bombs on

Hiroshima and Nagasaki. Another was Stalin's declaration of war against Japan on August 9. (That may have had an even greater effect on the Japanese than the bombs.) On August 15, the emperor addressed his people in an unprecedented radio broadcast, announcing surrender. There had been one attempt by fanatical Japanese army men to destroy the recording of the emperor's speech, but they had failed. Obedience and relief was the overwhelming response of the Japanese population. Constitutional monarchy saved the Japanese people from a great deal of further suffering (as it had saved much of the Italian people, and then the Greeks, in 1943 and 1944). Its absence had not saved the Germans. For them, 1945 was "Jahr Null," Year Zero.

12

THE DIVISION OF EUROPE
ALMOST COMPLETE

Europe still the center of history—The new geography of the continent—The movements of people—Rigidification of the division of Europe—The "iron curtain"—First American reactions—Truman Doctrine and Marshall Plan—Europe the center of the Cold War—Stalin and Asia

SOME OF MY READERS MAY question—justifiably—why until now this "short history of the twentieth century" has dealt principally with the history of Europe (and of the United States and the Soviet Union), with not much attention to the histories of other continents and peoples. After the twentieth century, not only the old predominance but also the preeminence of Europe may no longer exist. But the two world wars *and* then the Cold War, 1914–1989, were still mainly fought and decided in Europe. So it may be argued that even in view of the enormous political and geographic consequences of these world wars on other continents, Europe still remained the center of world history—due to the Cold War with its protagonists, the United States and the Soviet Union, until 1989.

By the end of the Second World War, in 1945, the political geography of Europe had already changed—though less so than after the First World War. Most of these changes were codified by a few treaties signed in 1947. The only substantial change was the reduction and division of Germany, the moving of Poland westward, and a few accretions on the borders of the Soviet Union. But far more important than these alterations of frontiers was the actual division of Europe—the way in which some of the central and much of the eastern portions of the continent fell under Russian rule.

The geographic limits of that rule, the essence of the division of Europe, were largely set even before the actual end of the war. By and large, with a few exceptions, Europe—and within it, Germany, and within Germany, Berlin—were divided along the lines where, near or at the end of the war, the Austrian and American and British armies had met. Even before that, in July 1944, Soviet and American and British delegations had agreed on the occupation zones allotted to each (a French occupation zone, carved out of the American one, was added a few months later); a similar zone agreement concerning Austria was made in January 1945. All of this was regarded as necessary in order to avoid conflicts— and also as temporary, which it was not. At the end of the war, in some parts of central Germany, American troops had met their Russian allies within the latter's zones. On July 1, 1945, the Americans retired behind their zonal boundaries; and American and British regiments were allowed to enter the city districts allotted to them in Berlin and Vienna. Less than a month later, the Second World War was over. There were still many influential American public officials and leaders of American opinion who were loath to think that a great and grave potential political conflict was looming between the Soviet Union and the United States. Harry Truman was not among them. It took a year until it became more and more obvious that such a conflict was actual.

Meanwhile, across Central and Eastern Europe, vast movements of peoples were occurring, transforming the ethnic geography of Europe. At least three million Germans fled westward before the Russian conquest of their homelands. Another three or four million were expelled from Czechoslovakia and Poland. Other hundreds of thousands left their lands and dwellings in Yugoslavia and Romania. This flood of migration went on for at least two years. It was probably one of the most enduring results of the Second World War. For the first time in centuries—in some places, after almost one thousand years—there were now practically no Germans left in Eastern Europe, beyond the new borders of what became the East German state. And after about 1947, for the first time in a millennium there were more Jews in the Western Hemisphere than in Europe and Russia.

The question, or problem, was not the existence of a Russian sphere of interest in Eastern Europe, but its conditions. What would Stalin do with it? What would it mean? A contrast, replete with sinister meanings, was already real in August 1944. Compare the Russian and American decisions when it came to the respective liberations of Warsaw and Paris. The Russians were not displeased to witness, across Warsaw, the German extirpation of the Polish Home Army, since the latter were not Communists; the Americans, out of goodwill, allowed de Gaulle's Free French to play a large part in the liberation of Paris, even though de Gaulle was not unquestionably pro-American. Soon after the end of the war, there was more evidence that Stalin wanted to seal off his portion of Europe from the West almost entirely. Churchill, long before others, was anxious and troubled about what that would mean. His powers were very limited; in August 1945, he and his party lost the British elections in a landslide victory for Labour. Still, he took it upon himself to speak up. In

March 1946 he traveled to Fulton, Missouri, to make his Iron Curtain speech. He warned America and the West that an "iron curtain" was descending from the Baltic to the Adriatic, a rigid barrier separating the continent of Europe in two. President Truman accompanied Churchill to Fulton with much sympathy and goodwill, though Washington was not yet ready to take steps to oppose the Russians.

––––––––––

But these would come, and soon. By the end of 1946, Moscow began to threaten Turkey, trying to detach a province of Iran; meanwhile, the Greek Communists renewed their civil war against the elected Greek regime. Truman sent two impressive warships through the Dardanelles and the Bosphorus, to the entrance of the Black Sea; and in February 1947, he announced what would be called the Truman Doctrine: an American commitment to defend the independence of Turkey and Greece. There followed the Marshall Plan, named after George Marshall, the highly respected general and then secretary of state: America's generous offer of funds and goods to repair the ravaged material conditions of European states. (The offer was extended even to states in the Russian sphere, but their governments refused.) The purpose of the Marshall Plan was, of course, to contain a further advance of Communism. In part, because of the wartime prestige of the Soviet Union, Communist parties were strong in some Western European countries such as France and Italy, but never strong enough to acquire power. Indeed, throughout the entire Cold War—forty years or more—there was not a single European country west of the Iron Curtain that went Communist. But by 1947, the so-called Cold War, the confrontation of the United States and the Soviet Union, had begun (even though the term "Cold War" was not invented by some American public thinkers until a year later).

It is remarkable that at the same time, the establishment of Stalin's "totalitarian" empire in Eastern Europe had its troubles even at that early stage of the Cold War. In some of the countries under his sway, elections in 1945 and 1946 did not bring Communist majorities. But the hope that Stalin would be content with unquestionably pro-Russian but not necessarily Communist regimes in Eastern Europe did not come about. Perhaps because of his own sense of insecurity, he thought it safest to force Communist rulers on Eastern Europe—governments run by people who were his toadies, without any doubt. By 1947 and 1948, such regimes were installed everywhere in that portion of Europe; Czechoslovakia was the last, in February 1948. This went together with the erection of an actual Iron Curtain: electrified wire fences, with watchtowers and minefields close to the fences, all along the frontiers separating Eastern from Western Europe. Stalin saw this as necessary, even with the executions and incarcerations of national Communists whom his and his satellites' secret police deemed at least potentially unreliable. Yet as early as 1948 came the first break in the Soviet Union's monopoly rule in Eastern Europe. In Yugoslavia, the Communist Josip Broz Tito had won something like a civil war, resulting in his brutal rule throughout that fissiparous country in 1945, with little Russian help. By 1948, Russian agents were denouncing him to Stalin for constructing a state without consulting the Soviet Union. Stalin immediately declared Tito a heretic and had him read out of the fraternity of Communist states. In part because of his somewhat favorable geographic situation, Tito did not give in.

In Germany, still at the center of Europe and thus at the center of the Cold War, the last indifferent attempts to seek some agreement between East and West, between the Soviet Union and the United States—attempts that were aimed at a peace treaty with Germany—ceased in 1947. After that, it became evident that there would be two German states, a Western (non-Communist) one and an Eastern (Communist) one, with the capital of the latter in East Berlin, which was likewise divided into halves (though without entirely impassable barriers between them). The two separate states were now recognized by their respective allies; and for a time, that was it. By 1949, the division of Europe was almost complete. That year, the permanent military presence of the United States in Europe was made official by the formation of the North Atlantic Treaty Organization. A dangerous peak period of the Cold War was to follow.

Europe (especially Germany) was still at the center of what was then contemporary history. Stalin knew this. His interest in the Far East, indeed in the Western Hemisphere, was limited. In 1945, he had agreed that the United Nations should be established in New York. After his entry into the war against Japan, and the latter's surrender, he requested that the Soviet Union occupy one of Japan's four main islands—a demand that Truman rejected, and that was the end of it. As late as 1947, Stalin did not object to the American accretion of former Japanese islands in the western Pacific—that is, the American domination of the Pacific. In 1948, he instantly recognized the establishment of the new State of Israel. The same year, a division of Korea rigidified into two countries, the north a Russian satellite, the south supported by the United States.

Stalin did not think much of China as a Great Power, though during the war he accepted Roosevelt's proposition that it was. Meanwhile, a Chinese civil war between Chiang Kai-shek's nationalists and Mao Tse-tung's Communists was developing. The

United States gave much support to the former; the Russians little to the latter. In 1945, they occupied parts of Manchuria, but then left it. From Japan, the Soviets got the southern half of the island of Sakhalin; and from China, a naval base on the China Sea. In 1947, General Marshall, then the American secretary of state, went to China to try for a mediated settlement between the Chinese nationalists and Communists, but in vain. By 1950, the Chinese Communists had won the struggle for China. Chiang and his remaining supporters fled to the island of Formosa, now Taiwan.

All of this (and the news that by 1949 Russia had exploded its first atomic bomb) had a profound effect on American politics, strategy, and popular sentiment. Communism now seemed the greatest power on the globe; next door to Russia, China and a large portion of Eurasia could be, and were, colored red. Then the first war between Communist and non-Communist states in the Far East began.

13

THE BRAVE HARRY TRUMAN

The Cold War at its peak—The Korean War—Death of Stalin—The Soviet Union begins to retreat—American misunderstandings—Russia and China—The so-called Third World emerges—The Cuban Missile Crisis—The tensions of the Cold War lessen

"INTERNATIONAL RELATIONS" IS AN inaccurate and often false term, in spite of its widespread employment in the twentieth century, the creation of institutions devoted to its study, and the high positions and prestigious academic degrees awarded by its representatives. It is a misnomer, because what almost all of them are talking about are not relations between nations but relations between states. This is so about many things (including the United Nations—which is not an organization but an inadequate assembly, and not of nations but of states). It is true that, especially in the democratic age (but also throughout all history), relations between nations can be very important, at times filling up the more or less traditional and actual framework of the relations between states. But the essence even of the Cold War, that peculiarly twentieth-century phenomenon, was that of the relations between two giant states, between the Soviet Union and the United States—not between Communism and Capitalism, or between Totalitarianism and Democracy, or between Atheism and Godliness, and so on, even though public opinion and popular sentiment played roles in that global conflict, to the extent of influencing and forming the relations among states. Their influences—indeed, factors—were more important in the conduct of American world policy during the Cold War than in that of the Soviet Union. To this I will return in Chapter 14; but here I must sum up, briefly, the state of Soviet-American relations during and after the peak of the Cold War.

It is true that during this period, the practices of the relations among states worsened to levels unknown and unprecedented in the Modern Age. This was the result of a choice made by the leadership of the Soviet Union and of its recent satellite states. Travel between them and non-Communist states and countries was cut to a minimum. So was what remained of international trade. Within these countries, the embassies and legations of non-Communist states were isolated by secret-police personnel, and the routine movements of their staffs were restricted to limits hitherto unseen. The anti-Western and especially the anti-American propaganda of these officially Communist and internationalist states was abysmal, and to a large extent unbelievable. Foreign citizens who remained in these states were at times imprisoned without cause. These states were kept closed from most of the rest of the world, in international as well as interstate relations.

Offensive behavior and defensive behavior may be opposites, yet they often overlap. Occasionally, their motives include suspicion and fear. So it is neither one-sided nor exaggerated to suggest that suspicion and fear may have been prime inclinations in the behavior of the Soviet Union during the Cold War, especially during its peak. And here we must pay necessarily brief attention to Stalin—in almost every way the very opposite of Karl Marx, who had been contemptuous of states, proclaiming that sooner or later they would entirely disappear. Stalin was a statesman of sorts, not a revolutionary. He had no interest in the Communist parties of, say, France or Italy or even Greece. His main interest at the end of the Second World War and during the Cold War was to retain, by every possible means, the sphere of Eastern European states allotted to him. But he must have understood, too, the (to him) unpleasant truth spoken by Churchill to de Gaulle in November 1944: the Russian wolf had a big appetite, but after the meal would come the digestion problem. Stalin, the realist statesman, was aware of that before others. For something like a Soviet retreat from parts of his Eastern European sphere had already begun before Stalin's death in March 1953, during and even before the peak of the Cold War. In 1948 he chose to break with Tito, but stopped short of a military move against Yugoslavia. In the same year (this, in my view, is more significant), he concluded a treaty with Finland—whose military virtues he respected—that allowed the latter, alone among the Eastern European states, to maintain a fair amount of independence. (The Finns, wisely, advised their neighbor Sweden not to become a member of NATO.) Later in 1948, the Soviets tried to restrict or force out the Western presence in West Berlin through a kind of blockade, closing most of the latter's land communications with West Germany. The Western Powers, foremost among them the United States, responded by feeding and supplying their half of Berlin through an airlift—very successfully. In 1949, the Soviets ended their blockade of Berlin.

Then on June 25, 1950, a real war broke out in Korea. The

armies of North Korea invaded the South. We still do not know whether this was a decision approved primarily by Stalin or by Mao Tse-tung, who had just won his civil war in China. In any event, they misread the Americans. There was only a small American military presence in South Korea, which was not officially part of the American defense system in the Far East, as were Formosa (Taiwan) and Japan. So either Mao or Stalin, or both, believed that their satellite North Korea could invade the South without an American military response. They were wrong. Much credit is due to the brave President Harry Truman, who immediately ordered American troops—and, more important, naval forces—to sustain the South Koreans. For a while the North Koreans streamed ahead, but soon an American amphibious invasion, planned and sustained by General MacArthur, reversed all that. Soon, Americans were well within North Korea, approaching the borders of China. The rulers of the latter responded by sending masses of Chinese soldiery against them. Eventually something like an armistice line formed largely along the previous border, the thirty-eighth parallel. A final armistice was made two years later, when Stalin was already dead. He had no intention of giving the North Koreans substantial help; conversely, the Americans kept well away from the Russian-Korean border. As a result of the war, North Korea, originally a Russian satellite state, became a Chinese satellite. Another long-range result: during the Cold War, the Korean War was the first American military involvement on the Asian continent. Other such American involvements would follow elsewhere, with dubious results; but in this instance, Harry Truman's decision in June 1950 had been the right one.

In March 1952, Stalin proposed a stunning change in the division of Europe—concerning primarily Germany—that did not receive the attention it deserved. He proposed a unification of the two Germanies, the removal of all foreign (Russian and American) troops and military installations from the Germanies, the abolition of all German military alliances, an essentially all-German army, and free German elections. It is possible that this was a shrewd move, with no other purpose than to sow confusion among the German people and prevent a German alliance with the United States. Such an alliance was Stalin's principal fear; but he may have intended his proposal seriously, as a basis for important negotiations. We cannot be sure. In any case, the Western Powers—foremost the United States, and West Germany under the chancellorship of Konrad Adenauer—rejected Stalin's note instantly, without any hesitation. Even bereft of any result, this had been a significant move by Stalin, who was ailing and probably unsteady. In less than a year he was dead.

He was succeeded first by Georgy Malenkov, then by Leonid Brezhnev and Nikita Khrushchev, with increasing power and authority going to the latter. The changes that were taking place in the Soviet Union's foreign relations were perhaps even more significant than its domestic changes, which included an astonishing speech by Khrushchev in 1956 in which he chastised Stalin for some of his dictatorial brutalities. Even before that, the Soviet Union had begun to retreat. It recognized the existence of, and established more or less normal relations with, the government of West Germany, without requiring that the Western Powers, including the United States, offer such recognition to the East German Communist state. It returned a Russian naval base to Finland, and two other Russian possessions in China to the Chinese government. It gave up the Russian occupation zone in Austria in exchange for the removal of all foreign troops there, thus establishing Austria's neutrality and independence. Khrushchev established normal relations with Yugoslavia and other European countries. He tried to improve relations with the United States (whose government, under President Dwight Eisenhower, was largely indifferent to the meaning of such changes, at least for some time). Meanwhile, a workers' revolt in East Germany, soon after Stalin's death in 1953, made that regime tremble in its boots; the revolt had to be suppressed with Soviet military help. In October 1956 (after Khrushchev's abovementioned speech), a near-revolt broke out in Poland, which quieted down after concessions were made by the Polish Communist Party and the government, with Wladislaw Gomulka, a popular and patriotic member, becoming its leader.

Less than a week later Hungary underwent a full-scale revolution during which Imre Nagy, another patriotic and well-liked party figure, became the nation's leader. In the end, he went so far as to declare Hungary's withdrawal from the alliance of Communist states in Eastern Europe. For several days and nights, the Soviet leaders in Moscow were in a state of near-panic. They announced and began the removal of Soviet troops from Hungary (perhaps even hoping for a reciprocal withdrawal of American forces from a Western or Southern European state). But this did not happen, and they had to change their minds. On November 4, the Soviet military reoccupied Budapest and the rest of Hungary. Nagy and most of his government were arrested and tried, and executed two years later. Almost 200,000 Hungarians fled to the West (whose governments thought it best to do nothing, save for issuing self-righteous condemnations of the Russians). Another—though minor—factor in their passivity was a contemporaneous crisis in the Middle East, involving Britain and France, Egypt and Israel, and the Suez Canal. The Soviets declared their support of Egypt, but in reality did little or nothing. (They even sided with the Americans in this instance, against Britain and France.) The Suez Crisis, like the Hungarian Revolution, blew over in a few weeks, though the Cold War did not.

The American public saw Russia's problems and reactions in Eastern Europe as yet further confirmation of the inherent and inevitable characteristics of that monstrous Communist state. The power of the latter seemed to be confirmed by the first successful Russian foray into space (the so-called Sputnik) in 1957. Worrisome, too, was Khrushchev's reopening of the Berlin problem in 1958. In contrast to their reaction ten years earlier, the Russians now attempted to reach some kind of settlement with the Western Powers through four-power negotiations, but in vain. A crisis involving East Berlin suddenly reached its zenith in August 1961, when the East German government (with the uneasy agreement of a reluctant Khrushchev) closed the small but still open gap between West and East Berlin, through which many thousands of East Germans had been fleeing to the West each year. A huge and monstrous wall was quickly built, separating the two halves of the city—additional evidence of Communist brutality. Yet this ugly decision by the East German government was, again, defensive rather than offensive: if that last gap within Berlin were to remain open, a large and unstoppable drain of the East German population would have gone on and on.

More telling is the date of that wall construction: August 1961. For by that time, relations between West and East, and especially between the United States and the Soviet Union, had improved. A few months earlier, the new American president, John Kennedy, had met Khrushchev in Vienna. Their meeting was inconclusive (as President Eisenhower's 1959 meeting with Khrushchev in Washington had been), but the atmosphere of this second summit was better. Even more important: at the very time when the wall closing up East Berlin was built, there was increasing evidence that elsewhere in Eastern Europe the "iron curtain" had begun to rust, with more and more small holes appearing in it. Commercial, travel, intellectual, and even a few political contacts between some of the states of Eastern Europe and the West were becoming more frequent.

But even more significant than the sporadic rusting of the "iron curtain" was the beginning of the end of the Two-Power World, where everything, or almost everything, depended on the relations between the two superpowers, the United States and the Soviet Union. I write "beginning" because in 1961 it was still too early to speak of a Third World—though two decades later that would become something more than a rhetorical reality, and within another decade the predominance of the Two-Power World would weaken, along with the Cold War. The spread and the popularity of anticolonialism, together with the propagation of nonalignment—meaning, in essence, the importance of Asia and Africa, comprising at least one-half of the population of the entire globe—had their national and intellectual origins earlier. They moved toward something like a reality in the 1950s, with the Bandung Conference of "nonaligned states" in 1955 and with other such conferences that followed. The development of all of this, including the notion of the Third World, was, of course, a consequence not so much of the vague and imprecise rhetoric of anticolonialist and "anti-alignment" conferences, as of the ending of an entire era—during which the European powers abandoned their colonies, mostly in the early 1960s. I will return to this soon; but before I do, let us note the crucial centrality of Europe as late as 1961, when, for instance, a slight shift of the boundaries of West Berlin to the east or a slight shift of the boundaries of East Berlin to the west, involving perhaps hardly more than a few dozen square miles, would have had world-political consequences far more important than events occurring in entire other continents at that time.

Yet the political preeminence of Europe—and, with it, that of the Two-Power World and even the Cold War—would not last very long. Indeed, it could be argued that as early as the 1950s a Third-Power World had come into existence, the Third Power being China. The leaders and shapers of the Bandung Conference in 1955 invited, cajoled, and welcomed Communist China as a "nonaligned" state, which was as inaccurate as many of the other formulations and declarations of that assembly. But their calculations were not without substance, since soon it appeared that there were plenty of troubles between the two Communist powers, China and Russia. When Khrushchev visited Washington in 1959, one of the discreet but important matters on his agenda was to impress upon President Eisenhower the possibility of American-Russian collaboration against China. Eisenhower, who took no pleasure and little interest in Khrushchev's visit, did not respond (just as he declined to respond to other Khrushchovian *ballons d'essai*). Less than eleven years later, it was President Richard Nixon who embarked on a definite course to improve American-Chinese relations, culminating in his pomp-laden journey to China, where he embraced Mao Tse-tung.

By that time, the Cold War between America and Russia was fading. But there were still episodes when it flared perilously high again, only to subside as rapidly as it had risen. One was the unexpected crisis involving Cuba in 1962. Four years before that, a brief revolution in Cuba had ended the rule of the pseudo-dictator, Fulgencio Batista. A young radical, Fidel Castro, now got into power. His political ideas and ideals were confused and weird. One fundamental feature of his inclinations was his dislike of the United States. (For a while he established and maintained very good relations with Franco's Spain.) In 1959 he wished to visit Eisenhower in Washington, an invitation that the American president refused to consider. Castro looked for other opponents of the United States to support his regime. The obvious choice (for him) was Communism and the Soviet Union. The latter was cautious. Castro's repeated urgings for a Cuban alliance with Russia were ignored. Meanwhile, his declarations in favor of Communism and the establishing of his local dictatorship went on and on (in a state less than one hundred miles from the United States—indeed, one whose very existence had been made possible by the latter hardly more than sixty years before). By 1962, it was obvious that the Kennedy administration in Washington was inclined to get rid of Castro. An American effort to support a guerrilla invasion in Cuba's Bay of Pigs in 1961 had failed. There were more and more signs that, for all kinds of reasons, President Kennedy was considering drastic moves, including a possible large-scale invasion of Cuba.

Castro, panic-stricken, implored Moscow for help. Khrushchev, after some serious soul-searching, thought he had to do something. Though he was still unwilling to declare a Russian alliance with Cuba, he chose to give Castro some weapons. Russia would ship missiles to Cuba, but under certain conditions: they would be medium-range rockets, capable of reaching only the southern parts of the United States; they would be equipped, manned, and controlled not by Cubans, but exclusively by Russian military technicians; and they would be shipped in Russian vessels starting from ports 5,000 miles away from Cuba, stacked on open decks, visible to American ships and aircraft. In mid-October 1962—when an American expeditionary force was also being assembled in southern Florida—the United States responded. President Kennedy declared a quarantine of Cuba. By October 24, American naval vessels and airplanes were approaching the first missile-bearing ships, whose cargo was clearly visible on board. The Russian vessels turned around. Two days later, the Russians proposed the sort of quid pro quo agreement that was customary for them: they would withdraw their missiles and bases (and their few airplanes) from Cuba, if the Americans would withdraw some of their missile bases from northern Turkey, near the southwestern Soviet Union. The American government agreed, though it refused to admit this reciprocal deal to the American people; but this did not matter. Soon, the quarantine against Cuba was lifted. The Russian missiles and personnel left the island soon after.

This was the last dangerous confrontation of the Cold War between the two superpowers. During the next twenty-five years, there were conflicts of lesser importance between them, but the Cold War largely faded. One consequence of the Cuban Missile Crisis was the removal of Khrushchev from the leadership of the Soviet Union in 1964. There were American presidents and politicians who, on occasion, were still inclined to see such conflicts as evidence of the historical struggle between Democracy and Communism, or even between good and evil. Yet that would matter less and less—especially when both the United States and the Soviet Union had to face all kinds of developments in the so-called Third World.

14

AMERICAN NATIONALISM, AMERICAN BENEVOLENCE

America's century: more than that—Problems rather than periods—Changes in the composition of the American people—Uniqueness during and after the Second World War—American nationalism—The emergence of American "conservatism"—The United States toward the end of the Cold War

THE UNITED STATES WAS ON its way to becoming the greatest power in the world even before 1914; but afterward it grew into that position and remained there. The period 1914–1989 was both the historical twentieth century *and* an American century—not only because the United States won both world wars and the so-called Cold War, but because its influence throughout the world in war and peace grew to affect the lives and habits of more and more countries and their peoples. This presents a problem almost beyond the competence of any serious historian, since the theme of America's relations with the rest of the world is enormous—especially in the twentieth century.

In 1914 most Americans, indeed the vast majority, took an interest in the spectacle of the war developing in Europe but had no inclination to wish the United States involved in it. Hardly more than two years later, this was no longer so. There had been a tectonic shift in American public opinion and popular sentiment, to a degree almost unprecedented in American history. In 1914, most Americans took pride in comparing their progressive and democratic country to Old Europe, which was once again in the throes of a great war. By 1917, most of them had convinced themselves that it was America's duty to set the Old World aright. By 1915, there were 100 million Americans. A historical coincidence: Americans had just completed the building of the Panama Canal, another gigantic engineering feat associated with the United States in the minds of more and more people around the world.

Because of an unusual split within the Republican Party in 1912 between William Taft and Theodore Roosevelt, the president of the United States was no longer the impressive Theodore Roosevelt, but Woodrow Wilson, whose view of the world was less realistic than that of his predecessor. Yet toward the end of the First World War, some of Wilson's ideas changed the map of Europe; moreover, they had a lasting influence within the United States as well. The propagation of national self-determination, and the first establishment of something like a world government—the League of Nations—was due to Wilson. No matter what their shortcomings, they remained instruments of American world policy long after Wilson.

Still, regardless of who was president, the American entry into the great European War in 1917—a reversal of America's chosen path after more than one hundred years—contributed in many ways to the predominance of the United States as the greatest world power. Meanwhile, America's losses in the war were a small fraction of the casualties that the European warring states had suffered.

Thereafter Wilson's influence in Europe waned, along with his popularity among the American people. Beginning in 1920, the Republicans won election after election. Nevertheless—despite mediocre Republican presidents, despite the repudiation of American interventions in Europe—in the 1920s America was on top of the world. So many of today's practices and ideas—ranging from the tolerance of sexual freedom to innovations in architecture, the arts, literature, music, and decoration—are adaptations of "new" things which appeared in the 1920s (whence, for instance, the designation "postmodern" is almost devoid of meaning). Many of these innovations originated in the United States.

The theme of this chapter is America and its relation to the world—the reciprocal effects they had on each other. Politically, the influence was still very slight; but in many other fields of life, America's effects on Europe were broad and often deep, permeating all levels of society, including widespread tastes for American music and movies. The influence of American popular culture grew, especially in Europe, far beyond the Twenties.

By the end of the Thirties, when the grave clouds of another European War began to gather, many people were openly expressing interest (and in some quarters hope) in America's reaction to the impending crisis. Thus, in the history of the world, 1939 differed significantly from 1914: what the United States would do now was very important.

Franklin Roosevelt's great contribution to the American people, in 1933 and after, was the radiation of his confidence. To a large extent, the same can be said about his image abroad. No

American president since Lincoln had such an image, not in Europe or in Asia. By 1939, millions of Europeans (and Chinese) knew that Roosevelt's America leaned toward and indeed stood by the adversaries of Hitler. In the Far East, Roosevelt supported the Chinese Nationalists, while he and his navy were acutely aware of the aggressive designs of the Japanese. (He was a navy man from the very beginning of his career—a condition that worked well for him and for American strategy, at least during the first years of the Second World War.) In 1940, he made two decisions that were crucial for the history of the war—indeed, for the entire world. First, by June, he had made it evident that no matter what happened in Western Europe, his United States would support Churchill's Britain. The other decision—less well-known but equally important—he arrived at in November 1940 (together with Admiral Stark). If the United States were to face a two-front war, in the Atlantic as well as in the Pacific, against Germany and against Japan, the first must have priority. The defeat of Germany had to come before the defeat of Japan. And so it was.

As the war went on, Roosevelt was fully aware (and so, probably, were most of the American people) that the United States was now the supreme power in the world. By 1942 or early 1943, he had concluded that the Soviet Union was the second-greatest power, and that consequently his relations with Stalin were even more important than his relations with the British government. There was some reason for such an assessment during the war, but not in the longer run. Roosevelt died on April 12, 1945, eighteen days before Hitler. The next day, Stalin ordered the Soviet newspapers to report Roosevelt's death on their front pages, which were to be printed with black borders to signify mourning. This did not mean a great deal, since the Cold War had already begun to form in the eastern half of Europe (to which Roosevelt had refused to pay much, if any, attention).

In 1945, the U.S. Navy was probably larger than all of the other navies in the world together. At that time, the gold reserves of the United States amounted to two-thirds of the gold reserves of the entire world. Americans and their country were generous after the war, as they had often been before. They gave large amounts of aid to their recent enemies—the Germans, the Italians, the Japanese—and even more to other European countries, their allies during the war. The so-called Marshall Plan, in 1947, was part and parcel of that. Stunning, too, is that the United States was still hardly dependent on profits from the exports of its tremendous industrial and agricultural production: more than 80 percent of what America produced was consumed by its own people.

This kind of national prosperity, despite gradual inflation, was changing American society. Class differences were melting away. (Americans of English or Scottish origin already accounted for less than 17 percent of the population, though until about 1950 they were still leaders of many traditional American institutions.) "Upper class," "middle class," and "working class" were terms still in general use, but they made less and less sense. The lower classes were gradually seeping into the upper. This social mobility was geographic as well as social; many Americans were moving west and south. That was not unusual in American history, but something else was also happening. During the twentieth century, not only the rural, agricultural period but also the "bourgeois," urban period of American history was ending. After about 1880, the great cities of America grew very fast. Young, eager, and socially and intellectually ambitious people aspired to live in these great cities, discarding what seemed to be constrained, parochial, provincial habits of living and thinking. That was not universally true; but "urban" and "urbane" then had largely the same approbatory meaning. Soon after 1945, this tendency weakened. It became possible for many, indeed most, Americans to acquire small, detached properties, comprising a house and garden, outside the cities, though not too distant from them. Suburbs, once bridges between city and country, now began to devour both. By the mid-1950s, an average American was no longer urban, but suburban. This had many consequences, such as the later tendency of many American wives to seek employment outside their homes.

What did not cease or weaken was American nationalism, but it found new outlets during the initial years of the Cold War. From 1945 to 1947, the wartime and occasionally excessive appreciation of Americans for their Soviet allies changed to an anxious hostility. The reason for this was simple: it was the behavior of the Russians themselves. But it had a few, perhaps typical, American consequences: to see the world, especially America's adversaries, ideologically more than geographically or politically. The overwhelming popular—and often public—belief was that the great danger to America and to the world was Communism. There was a brief precedent for this in 1920–1922, after the First World War and the Bolshevik Revolution (then called the Red Scare), but after 1947 the fear was much more powerful, pervasive, and long-lasting. It had some regrettable consequences. On occasion, it influenced and impeded America's foreign policy and some of its presidents. It also led to a popular preoccupation with domestic Communist sympathizers and their fellow travelers, whose influences had existed, though they were minimal, especially after 1947. The harm that their ambitious prosecutors, such as Senator Joseph McCarthy, did to American constitutional liberties was worse than regrettable, but it did not last long. What persisted longer was the ideological element, which lasted throughout much of the rest of the Cold War. Americans who viewed the world through an ideological lens were unable or unwilling to consider the problem of the Soviet Empire as different from that of international Communism.

This included the emergence and rise of the American "conservative" movement, beginning very soon after 1950. American public figures, including just about all American politicians, eschewed that adjective for a very long time. But now came a change. "Conservative" now meant to be fixedly and rigidly anti-Communist. But it also meant a reaction against American liberalism and progressivism, which dominated much of American intellectual life and its institutions, surely in the 1930s and 1940s. There were reputable American thinkers, scholars, writers, even historians who, as late as the early 1950s, wrote serious books stating that there was only one American intellectual tradition: a liberal one. This was not so. A few intelligent, independent-minded writers and thinkers discovered and rediscovered American conservatives of the past, whether these had called themselves conservatives or not. But more effective for the rise of the conservative movement in the United States in the 1950s was the growing disaffection for the designation "liberal" (at least partly because of the excesses of American liberalism). Many of the now self-proclaimed American conservatives were really not very conservative at all. It is at least significant that as late as 1952, a rigid Republican conservative and nationalist such as Senator Robert Taft would still call himself an "old-fashioned liberal." Another ten years later, President Eisenhower, who continued many of the New Deal policies and expanded Social Security, on one occasion called himself a "conservative." Another ten years later, the majority of Americans voted for Richard Nixon, an out-spoken "conservative." Ten more years later, they voted for Ronald Reagan, some of whose statements were those of a radical conservative; among other things, he declared the Soviet Union an "evil empire."

Some of this mattered, but not very much. When the habits, lifestyles, and thinking of Americans changed, they did so in different ways. The so-called Youth Revolution of the 1960s, for example, produced rapid changes in behavior, clothing, music, entertainment, even social and sexual manners (or rather, their absence). There was commendable civil-rights legislation, promoted by President Lyndon Johnson in the mid-1960s, which benefited black Americans. Yet this same president, confident in the supremacy of American military power, kept extending its presence in Indochina; the result of that was the Vietnam War, which became less popular as it went on, and ended with a withdrawal. Other and more enduring problems for the United States had begun to appear. Gold had been trickling out from the American treasury, until in 1971 President Nixon forbade its availability to foreign borrowers. More important: domestic inflation in the United States was rising, and the international value of the dollar began to decline—while within the country, credit-card financing and its transactions grew to be nearly universal. Even more important: the composition of the American population was changing, mostly because of the increasing (and often uncontrollable) immigration of many people from countries to the south of the United States—a Hispanization of considerable portions of the republic, with many cultural and even political consequences. Yet none of these changing circumstances and conditions led to grave popular reactions—except, perhaps, that the once-accustomed categories of "liberal" and "conservative" had grown more and more inaccurate, losing their former meanings.

In 1980, it seemed—but only seemed—that the Cold War was reviving. Some of President Reagan's words and deeds seemed to indicate that. A "conservative" and an anti-Communist, he was also a former movie actor and a sentimental nationalist. This inclination could have been dangerous, had the great crisis of the Soviet Union not occurred at the same time. The "evil empire" had begun to break up about the time Reagan became president. During his second presidency (he was overwhelmingly reelected in 1984), even he recognized that the new Russian leader, Mikhail Gorbachev, was attempting to change not only the Soviet government, but its relations with its neighboring states—indeed, with the world. Eventually the two leaders had an amicable meeting. By the time Reagan boarded his presidential airplane to fly back to his beloved southern California, the Cold War was over.

After all, Reagan was an American. Despite his public pronouncements, despite all of the superficial and emotional essence of his American nationalism, he was not devoid of a certain benevolent tolerance. Nor, to a greater extent, were the American people. They had been willing to support and to cheer on what many foreigners saw as American "imperialism," but that was not the right word either. After all, America had lived through decades without attempting to turn the Cold War into the enormity of a real war with the Soviet Union. Americans did think that their country was the greatest and the best and the most powerful in the world—but that was that. There was an enduring element of American benevolence beneath or within the expanses of American self-confidence. "Beneath," or "within"? It did not matter. What mattered was yet another instance of this, when the entire Cold War, and with it the history of the entire twentieth century, came to an end. In general, the American people welcomed the transformations and the military and political withdrawals of the Soviet Union, without evidence of self-congratulation, with hardly any sense of victory.

15

"EUROPE," AND THE END
OF THE COLD WAR

"Europe": impreciseness of its definition—The principal object during the Second World War—After that, its division and the consequences—Attempts toward an integration of Europe—The decomposition of the Russian sphere in Europe—Its rapidity around 1989, while its consequences are not foreseeable

FOR THE LAST TIME IN this book, I must devote a chapter to Europe—in, and at the end of, the Cold War. My readers and critics may object to this Europe-centeredness, with good reason. This book bears the title *A Short History of the Twentieth Century.* But until now, I have said little or nothing about Africa, South America, Asia, and other parts of the world. In the twentieth century, their portion of the world's population grew enormously. After 1950, the population of Europe, including Russia, hardly rose at all—while the numbers of people in the rest of the world more than doubled. (The entire population of the globe was about 2.5 billion in 1950; in 1990, it was about 5.3 billion.) Why, then, this lopsided emphasis, this concentration on Europe in the twentieth century? My reasons are simple. The two world wars and then the Cold War involved mostly Europe; they were mostly fought in Europe; they were decided in Europe—probably the last time in history that a great war would be decided there. During the twentieth century, the primary importance of Europe still prevailed, though it had begun to fade. The twentieth century was an interim century—the end of an entire age, and most probably the beginning of a new age. But speculations about the latter are not within the province of this small book.

The very definition of "Europe" is more recent than we are accustomed to think. For long centuries the term was not widely used, save on certain occasions. Geographically, Europe is a large peninsula on the west of Asia. It was not until 1833 that a German geographer defined its eastern limits along a boundary that separated the "European" from the Asian portions of the Russian Empire. Regarding the Turkish Ottoman Empire, its possessions in southeastern Europe kept changing over the life of the empire. In 1914, within geographic Europe only a very small portion of Turkey remained, around Constantinople. Four years later, the Russian and German empires retreated from some of their Eastern European possessions, while close to the middle of Europe the Austro-Hungarian Empire broke into pieces, a result of which was the establishment of new Eastern European states. There was now a new and unstable eastern half of Europe. In 1914 the spark that was to ignite the First World War had risen from there; in 1939, Eastern Europe was in many ways the cause of the Second World War. Hitler wanted to dominate it; he knew that if he succeeded, the importance of the Western European powers would very much diminish. That was why in 1939 an anxious government in Britain, for the first time in its history, gave a British guarantee to an Eastern European state, Poland, hoping to convey to Hitler that he could go this far but no farther, and thus avoid a second European, indeed world, war. It did not succeed. Hitler turned to Stalin; they then divided Poland and other parts of Eastern Europe between themselves.

We know what resulted in 1945—or rather, until 1989. Before 1945, Britain and the United States depended on Russia in order to conquer Germany. Either Hitler would rule just about all of the continent; or Stalin, about half of it. The western half of Europe was better than none—but it was Stalin's practices and methods that brought the Cold War about. Worse: no one could be sure that Stalin would stop at the "iron curtain." The result was the American military and political commitment to protect Western Europe. Another result was the tendency of thoughtful Western Europeans to proceed to an integration, or possibly even a union, of Western Europe. Such a movement or desideratum existed faintly in the 1920s, but then was washed away by Hitler's conquests. Soon after 1946, it revived again, more widespread and important than the "pan-European" advocacies before the war. (One of their outspoken supporters was Churchill.) For fifty years after 1948, the establishment of a European institution advanced in successive steps. No need to list them in this little book, since they are well known: the European Coal and Steel Community, the European Common Market, the European Defense Community, the Schengen Plan (providing for unhindered travel within most of Europe), a common European currency, the euro.

Yet the plan for a united Europe had grave shortcomings, some of them from its very beginning. There was, at the outset, an emphasis on economic and financial matters, rather than on states and politics. In the late 1940s, there was a genuine desire, especially among the youth of some Western European states, for something like a political union. (The very first flag of the united-Europe movement showed a green "E" on a white field.

The later, still-existing flag of the Council of Europe is a rather uninspiring adaptation of the American stars, without stripes: a dozen stars in a circle in a dark-blue field.) There was a belief that economics must precede statecraft. Well, it did and it didn't. Forty or fifty years after 1948, there was no European government, no European executive power, no European army. Forty or fifty years after 1948, the enthusiasm and the attraction that young Europeans felt for a united Europe—indeed, for a particular identity in being European—had faded. Except here and there, most Europeans were unready to face the problems and challenges of a new situation: the end of the Cold War, the breakup of the Soviet Union—indeed, the end of the division of Europe. When, a mere two years after 1989, Yugoslavia broke up in a series of civil and tribal wars, "Europe" did nothing; shamefacedly, it allowed the United States to intervene in the Yugoslav problem by aerial bombing.

Near the end of and after the Second World War, considerable demographic changes occurred in Europe, the first phase of which affected mostly Germany. From 1945 to 1948, more than five million Germans fled or were expelled from Poland and Czechoslovakia (other, smaller groups followed them from portions of Yugoslavia, Romania, and other countries). These German refugees were absorbed into the prosperous society of West Germany with surprisingly little trouble, and soon without many political consequences. But after that, came another, more momentous and portentous change, now from the South rather than from the East. Beginning even before the end of the European overseas colonial empires, many hundreds of thousands of people started to move—some of them legally, others not—from the global South and East into Western Europe. They were preceded by other, sometimes temporary migrants (often Turks) seeking work in the great industrial plants, especially in Germany. After 1961, this movement of hundreds of thousands, even millions of people, mostly from North Africa and the Middle East, grew very large, with all kinds of social and political consequences whose end is unforeseeable.

After 1950, the United States, too, had to face a constantly increasing and mostly illegal immigration from the global South. The effects of this on the composition of American society and on American politics were, and continue to be, considerable. There are two main elements that distinguish the immigration experiences of America from those of Europe. First, the land mass of North America is much greater than Europe's, and able to accommodate new arrivals more easily. Second, the children of immigrants to North America assimilate more readily than the children of migrants to Europe's nations. Yet the great historical movement of the past five hundred years is now reversing. For five hundred years, people, most of them born in Western Europe, moved across oceans, spreading throughout and settling in other continents. Now many of their descendants have been returning from those places, while some people from Africa and Asia are pressing toward Europe.

Meanwhile, an event of very great importance was unfolding in Europe: the retreat of the Soviet Union. As early as 1961, the "iron curtain" began to show holes here and there (even though the Berlin Wall was then being built). Trade and travel restrictions and intellectual constraints were eased somewhat. These partial reforms were not ordained by Moscow; they almost always resulted from decisions by rulers of its satellite states. One-party states and rulers still existed, but there was palpable evidence of a desire for greater freedom among their peoples. One example of this was Czechoslovakia in 1968, where Alexander Dubček, a decent man and something of an idealist, was about to move the regime in the direction of a European democracy, without proclaiming so. The rulers in Moscow were worried. They chose to invoke the Warsaw Pact, a so-called alliance system of the satellite states of Eastern Europe, and invaded Czechoslovakia with tanks and troops. There were few casualties, and even Dubček was allowed to retire and live out his life. But that was not the end. Worker revolts erupted in Poznan, Poland, two years later, and recurred in 1976. In 1978, the Polish cardinal Karol Wojtyla was elected pope—he took the name John Paul II—an unprecedented elevation of very great importance, because of the exceptional qualities of this hierarch, but also because of its effects in Poland, where he went in 1979. (Would the Soviet Union have permitted his visit thirty years earlier? It would have been inconceivable.) About the same time, a new Polish workers' organization called "Solidarity" arose, a drastic break with the monopoly of the Communist Party and the state. Its popular success was such that in late 1981, the Polish minister of defense proclaimed martial law and arrested Lech Walesa, the leader of Solidarity— but without prosecuting him. Soon Solidarity (and Walesa) reappeared. The Soviet leadership had hesitated, choosing not to intervene.

But the Cold War was not yet over—mostly due to a new American president, Reagan, elected in 1980. During the Seventies it was possible and even current to speak of "détente" in Russian-American relations, one result of which was a general agreement signed in Helsinki in 1975, including cumbrous and indeterminate details. Even before 1980, the American government had been shocked by the Soviet decision to invade Afghanistan, whose new ruler had displeased Moscow. Within two years, the Russian-Afghan War was a failure and the Russians withdrew from that unpredictable and ungovernable country. But Reagan, comfortably convinced of the supreme doctrine of anti-Communism, was uninterested in improving American-Russian relations; indeed, he intervened militarily in the Caribbean Nicaragua, El Salvador, and the tiny island of Grenada against irresponsible governments and guerrilla movements which, though anti-American, were not and could not be considered springboards of the Soviet Union south of the United States. In 1983, Reagan also announced a New Defense Initiative (dubbed "Star Wars" by its critics) that, at least for a while, made American-Soviet disarmament agreements impossible.

But Reagan's "evil empire" was tottering, no matter what he believed or wished to believe. There were so many indications of this, that soon he had to change his mind. In March 1985, Mikhail Gorbachev became general secretary of the Communist Party and the leader of the Soviet Union (he was a protégé of Yuri Andropov, who, as Soviet ambassador to Hungary, had been an exceptionally shrewd observer of the Hungarian Revolution). Gorbachev proclaimed and then pursued "perestroika" and "glasnost," the former term meaning the (for him) unavoidable reforms of the Russian economy—indeed, of Russian society; the latter meaning the necessary opening of public opinion. Perhaps even more important was his conviction that the eventual success of these reforms depended on essential changes in Russian foreign policy, first of all in Russian-American relations. Soon after Gorbachev's assumption of power, the accumulated evidence and proof of these inclinations trickled down to Reagan, who now began to consider and even appreciate them. A result of this was the two leaders' first summit meeting, in Geneva in

November 1985. Three other summits followed, over the subsequent three years. In the end, Reagan and Gorbachev got along quite well.

All of this marked the end of the Cold War between the United States and the Soviet Union. But even more important than this significant improvement in Russian-American relations was the drastic change in Russia's relations with its neighbor states—indeed, the end of the "iron curtain" dividing Europe. Very soon after his assumption to power in 1985, Gorbachev advised the rulers of the Warsaw Pact states that they would have to control their own affairs, without intervention from the Soviet Union. This became more and more obvious. Less than three years later, one-party rule in Poland, Hungary, Czechoslovakia began to end. The year 1989 was, then, an *annus mirabilis.* In these countries, monopoly rule truly ended; there were free elections. Elsewhere in Eastern Europe, too: before the end of the year, the Berlin Wall was pulled down, and West and East Germany were reunited. All of this took place without any bloodshed (the only small exception was Romania).

Gorbachev himself declared that the Cold War was over. His problems were not. He was unpopular among Russia's politicians and with the Russian people at large, who felt or saw, rightly or wrongly, that he was responsible for the sudden decline of Russia as a great power. For what was happening now was something more than the end of Russia's domination of its European neighbors; it was the breakup of the Soviet Union itself. By early 1991, the former Baltic republics Estonia, Latvia, and Lithuania (since 1940 forcibly incorporated within the Soviet Union) had declared their independence. So did Ukraine, Belorussia, Moldova, and Azerbaijan. An attempt to overthrow Gorbachev failed. He resigned at Christmas. The new president was Boris Yeltsin, who declared the end of the Soviet Union and the birth of a new Russia, represented no longer by its red flag but by its ancient tricolor banner.

What would happen with Russia in the future is beyond the scope of this book. The consequences of the Soviet Union's breakup were, and may still be, enormous. Within Russia itself, the historic and ancient division between easterners and westerners, "Slavophiles" and "Westernizers," was temporarily disappearing. Still, one matter belonging to the twentieth century, including the Cold War, may be worth mentioning: after nearly a half-century of occupation by Russia, the effects of Russian culture, language, religion, and habits on the peoples of Eastern Europe were virtually nonexistent.

At the same time, many of the differences between Western and Eastern Europe continued and continue to exist.

The Cold War was over. The century of great European wars was over. The division of Europe was over. But so was the European Age, the primacy of Europe over the rest of the world.

16

"GREAT LEAP FORWARD"

The Third World—Near and Middle East—Far East and
Australia—Africa—South America and the Western Hemisphere—The movements of peoples

THE TERM "THIRD WORLD" HAS two meanings, one temporary and the other long-range. Its temporary—though still current—usage emerged around 1955, connected with the Bandung
Conference of that year, when leaders and spokesmen for Asian
and other countries declared that they represented a large portion of the world unaligned with and independent of the United
States and the Soviet Union, the two superpowers. The term
expressed something largely obvious but also inaccurate, since
neither a unified entity nor a political conglomeration called a
"Third World" came about. But the end of the Cold War neither
affected nor diminished its meaning. For many centuries, no one
spoke of a "Third World." Moreover, Europe and Russia expanded, establishing colonies on other continents and especially
in Africa. In some portions of the world, such as Australia and
New Zealand, British and Irish people conquered largely empty
continents and groups of islands. There, and in some of the states
of South America, that "whitening" of parts of the globe is still
apparent. Elsewhere, by and large, it is not.

During the twentieth century, the rule of European powers on other continents ceased to exist. Many kinds of new states filled the void after their departure. In South and Central America, this had already happened in the nineteenth century. In Africa, it occurred mostly in the twentieth. In the so-called Middle East, such a development was more complicated. There, and on the vast continent of Asia, ancient empires such as Iran (Persia), India, Japan, and China went on to exist in newer, centralized, transformed ways. One result of all of this was an enormous multiplicity of states within the United Nations—a Rooseveltian idea put into practice in 1945, with its headquarters a glass-covered pimple on the brute flank of New York, and by the end of the twentieth century one with little power or even meaning. What will happen with the history of "states" in the future, no one can tell. Recall only that in the so-called Modern Age, now passing, for at least five centuries the main instruments of politics and history were those of states and of their wars with one another. Whether this will form the structure of the history of peoples in the future is unanswerable.

A related question, answerable only with great uncertainty, is the origin of most of these states. It is at least possible to trace the origins—well, at least some of the origins—of "modern" France, "modern" Italy, "modern" Germany, and so on, if by "modern" we mean the existence of a largely unified French or Italian or German state that came into being sometimes at least five, in other cases less than two, centuries ago. Before and after that, a sense of nationhood began to fill up the framework of their states. The word "nationalism" hardly existed before the nineteenth century; but at least in Europe, the ideal of a national state (or, later, of "national self-determination") became dominant. But that ideal of a national state—indeed, the very consciousness of nationality, as something different from other habits of religious or racial or tribal identification, including self-identification—did not emerge in Asia or in Africa until sometime in the twentieth century. Before that, there were a handful of thinkers, writers, and ambitious politicians espousing something like it— but without much, or any, effect. It was the end of colonial rule by the "white" powers that—with notable exceptions, such as Japan—brought about Asian and African nationalism.

During and after the First World War, there were stirrings of nationalism and anticolonialism in the Near East, India, and China. The movement's prophet and leader, Mohandas Gandhi, had appeared in India. More and more Chinese were shocked and hurt to see how portions of their former empire had been surrendered to European powers and especially to Japan. In 1917, the British began to support Arab nationalism against the declining and receding Turkish Ottoman Empire. The status of Africa did not much change. There were only two more or less independent states throughout that enormous continent: Liberia in the west and Abyssinia (Ethiopia) in the east. In 1935, between the wars, Mussolini chose to invade and conquer the latter, whereby a large Italian empire came to exist in East Africa, comprising Abyssinia, Italian Eritrea, and Somalia. Five years later, British and Commonwealth troops put an end to that. Elsewhere, and especially in Far Eastern Asia, the Second World War led to the end of colonialism. The Japanese attempted to profit from this, and in many ways they did—in some countries and among some people, even with enduring results.

"Asia for Asians" was a Japanese slogan. In Indonesia, Burma, and even the Philippines, pro-Japanese nationalist and anticolonialist "independent" regimes came into existence; the Japanese also promoted an Indian nationalist movement, and in Southeast

Asia a small Indian National Army—but this army never got as far as India. During the Second World War, there were three competing regimes in China: that of Chiang Kai-shek in Chungking, closely allied with the Americans and the British; that of Mao Tse-tung's Communists, mostly in northwestern China; and that of Wang Ching-wei, promoted and supported by the Japanese in Nanking. It is telling that, with few exceptions (Wang among them), the pro-Japanese collaborationists after the war did not undergo anything like the punishment of the pro-Nazi collaborationists in Europe. One example: the pro-Japanese Sukarno in Indonesia went on to become its national leader immediately after the war. In sum, anticolonialism and nationalism have now become much the same thing—and throughout much of the Third World.

The most complicated and long-lasting consequences of the two world wars—further complicated by matters during the Cold War—were those in the "Middle East." This geographic term, too, requires some explanation. Before, say, 1945, there were the Near East and the Middle East, the first encompassing the states and the lands west of India; the latter, India and some of Southeast Asia west of the Far East. The term "Near East" has now disappeared, which may be geographically regrettable (though politically perhaps not), since the development and history of India during the past sixty years have differed from those of most states west of it—from what we imprecisely, but perhaps tellingly, call the Middle East.

The most important and enduring development in the Middle East began as early as the First World War. It was the breakup of the Turkish Ottoman Empire. Even before 1914, Turkish rule and sovereignty over much of it was feeble. By 1917, the British had pushed the Turks out of Palestine and other places; and they announced the so-called Balfour Declaration, which granted the Jews a homeland in Palestine after nearly 2,000 years. Six weeks before Germany, Turkey surrendered to the Allies. Its empire dissolved. But there arose a national hero and savior, Mustafa Kemal, capable of repairing at least the most senseless and injurious mutilations that had been imposed on Turkey in 1920 by the Allies, including Greece. The Treaty of Sèvres was revised in 1923 by the Treaty of Lausanne. By that time, Kemal had defeated and expelled the Greeks from their considerable enclaves in Turkey, which became a solid, stable, and almost homogeneous state, while conceding the cession of much of its erstwhile empire. This was one of the few historical examples in which the amputation of large, nonnational provinces turned out to be an unquestionable benefit for the mother country.

The British now held Palestine, where they had to be careful not to alienate the large Arab population. They tried to limit the immigration of large quantities of Jews into Palestine. The French established a protectorate over Syria and Lebanon. All of this would come to an end soon after the Second World War. During the war, in 1941, the British had to contend with a nationalist uprising in Iraq, which they defeated. Later that year, they and the Soviet Union together deposed the shah of Iran, elevating his son to the throne. Both of them now occupied northern and southern zones of that country. These became an important passageway for American armaments and supplies shipped to Russia. Soon after 1945, Iran was the site of a brief episode that foreshadowed the coming Cold War. In January 1946, the Russians tried to detach two of the northwestern provinces of Iran, keeping Soviet troops there. A year later, Stalin thought it better to give that up. By that time, the influence of the Americans in the Middle East had grown well beyond that of the British. One of the prime elements of this was the increasing importance of Middle Eastern oil, especially in Iran, Kuwait, and Saudi Arabia. From 1940 to 1950, Middle East production of oil increased about sixfold; another ten years later, it amounted to more than half of the world's oil production.

In 1951, after the leader of Iran was assassinated, a weird political personality, Mohammad Mosaddegh, forced the shah to make him the prime minister of Iran. Mosaddegh immediately nationalized the Iranian oil industry, expelling the British companies and their experts, who had been running it. In 1953, President Eisenhower and the CIA helped to organize Mosaddegh's overthrow and the restoration of the shah's authority. The United States thus replaced Britain's traditional primacy in supporting Iran's independence, besides being that country's principal Western economic ally. This did not matter much, at least not for a while. In the 1950s, the main contentions and troubles and even wars occurred in what was once called the Near East, involving many Arab states and nations (including Egypt), as well as Israel.

Many of the Arabs in the Middle East had a common language and a common religion, Islam. Their populations were increasing rapidly. Yet they were not united, and attempts at even partial unions failed. They *were* united against Israel because there was a large Arab population within Palestine. Soon after 1945, the British realized that their presence in Palestine/Israel had become useless. They, the United States, and even the Soviet Union agreed in 1947 to turn to the United Nations, which proposed that Palestine be partitioned into two states—one Jewish and the other Arab. The Arab states would not accept the existence of a Jewish state. In May 1948, the British left. Immediately, the Israelis declared the founding of a Jewish state. Immediately, the Arab states of Egypt, Syria, Transjordan, Lebanon, and Iraq attacked Israel. This war the Israelis won, even though they were outnumbered. They fought better than their enemies, whose armies were not unified. Eventually, something like a cease-fire came into being, though it was a very frail, incomplete thing.

In 1948, both the United States and the Soviet Union supported Israel. This did not last long, mostly because of the rising power of Arab nationalism and populism. In 1952, Egyptian military officers overthrew the monarchy of King Farouk; soon a former colonel, Gamal Abdel Nasser, was at the head of Egypt. He began to accept some armaments from the Soviet Union. In 1956, he declared the nationalization of the Suez Canal Company, which had been built and managed by France and Britain. The governments of these ancient powers, already buffeted and shorn by Arab nationalists here and there, concluded—after some hesitation, and against the American secretary of state, John Foster Dulles—that they had to make a stand. They included Israel in their plans. The latter would advance across the Sinai Peninsula toward the canal, stopping before it, while French and British naval and air forces would descend on the canal and seal it off from Egypt. It was a short, brilliant war. The Soviet Union threatened to intervene, without much effect. President Eisenhower did intervene, with considerable effect. After less than a week, the Israelis, the British, and the French withdrew. Less than two years later, a revolution put an end to the once pro-British monarchy in Iraq. Step by step, American troops were dispatched to various Middle Eastern countries, here and there.

No Arab country would accept the existence of Israel. There were no agreed-upon frontiers, only cease-fire lines between Israel and its neighbors. Israel was a viable state, and fairly prosperous; still, it had a population of fewer than three million, while its surrounding Arab countries had a combined population at least ten times that size. They formed a Palestine Liberation Organization; but in other ways, they were not united. In May 1967, Nasser threatened to close the southern mouth of the Sinai, choking off Israeli shipping, though perhaps not much more. The Israelis decided that this was a propitious time for a preemptive war. On June 5, they attacked Egypt, then followed this up with attacks on Jordan and then Syria. In less than six days, they defeated the armies of each. There was another ceasefire. Neither the Soviet Union nor the United States had intervened. The State of Israel now acquired considerable territories —but also a large Arab population in the West Bank, source of immediate and future troubles.

In October 1973, there was another short war between Egypt and Israel that ended in a draw. But meanwhile, the leaders of the Arab states, as well as those of Iran, realized that they had another important instrument not only for increasing their revenues, but also for influencing the Great Powers, including the United States. This instrument was their ability to control oil prices. They started by raising the price of their oil by about 70 percent. Soon, they tripled the price. But here is yet another example of how the effects of even the most radical and extreme economic and financial matters are much less severe than people usually think. These new and startling financial revenues changed little in the lives, or indeed the minds, of most people in these oil-producing states. Their political revolutions, with their populist and nationalist slogans and chiefs, mattered much more. The monarchies in Libya and Iraq were gone. More important was the case of Iran. Its shah was overthrown in 1979 by a revolutionary Islamic movement and its ayatollah (Khomeini). This, in

a state whose revenues had recently doubled or even tripled—
and where millions of people now drove automobiles.

One commendable development was a peace treaty signed by
Egypt and Israel in 1979, arranged by the American president,
Jimmy Carter. To this day, it has been the first and only such
treaty between Israel and one of its Arab neighbors, and was promoted by the president of Egypt, Anwar Sadat, who had succeeded Nasser. Sadat was assassinated two years later. The year
1989, when the Cold War ended, was not marked by any substantial change in the Middle East. Populist nationalism was still the
order (or the disorder) of the day, including the senseless radical
hostility of Iran against the United States.

The state and country of Afghanistan (not really part of the
"Middle" East) was attacked and invaded by Russia because of
the elimination of one supposedly pro-Communist ruler by another tribal chief; but the Russians, not for the first time in Af-
ghan history, were defeated and then withdrew. The United
States chose to send a portion of its army to Afghanistan later—
another senseless move. But by that time, not only the Cold War
but the historical twentieth century was over. In the Near East,
too, it had begun in 1914, but it did not all end in 1989. Populist
nationalism in the Middle East is still going on.

During the entire twentieth century, there was no real collision
between Russia and the United States across much of the vast
continent of Asia. During the chaos of the Bolshevik Revolution
and its ensuing civil war, Japan attempted to gain an important
foothold in the Russian Far East in 1920, but then it pulled back,
partly because of American pressure. We have seen that in 1945
the United States and Russia were, briefly, allies against Japan.

During the Korean War, both were careful to keep clear of each other. What seemed to becloud everything was the issue of Communism and China. Yet by 1989, China had become—sort of—a friend and a supplier of the United States, more and more capitalist, though officially Communist. Except for North Korea, rigidly Communist regimes all over Far Eastern and Southeastern Asia ceased to exist. There were now four great or considerable powers in Asia: China, India, a resurrected Japan, and Russia, with its imperial possessions in the north—a quadripartite geographic order quite unlike the situation in the Middle East or Africa, and not entirely different from the one that had existed in the past.

What had seemed (but only seemed) to change everything at the beginning of the Cold War was the triumph of the Communists in the civil war in China. Suddenly it looked as if more than half of the world had turned red. Yet Russia was still Russia, and China was China. There were conflicts between them from the beginning of the Cold War. Stalin preferred two Chinas, instead of one. Mao Tse-tung, the leader-dictator of the new Communist China, was not favorably disposed toward Stalin and Russia. Meanwhile, for more than twenty years, Mao's ideas and his rule did China no good at all. His collectivization and nationalization of Chinese agriculture and industry were bad enough; his doctrinal declarations "Let a hundred flowers bloom" (citizens were encouraged to express their views) and the "Great Leap Forward" (Mao's campaign for rapidly modernizing China's economy) were disasters, resulting in millions of deaths. The Soviet Union made a few geographic concessions to China in 1954–1955, but these did not really improve their relations. By the end of that decade, their mutual distrust was evident. Khrushchev denounced Russia's military agreements with China; during a border conflict between China and India, he declared that both countries were friends of the Soviet Union. Ten years later, Chinese and Russian armies fought for at least a month along the Ussuri River. Then President Nixon declared his friendship for China, visited Peking, and hugged the wizened and tottering Mao with both arms. Nixon thought that he was a great statesman playing the Chinese card. In reality, it was the Chinese who were playing the American card. Soon Mao died, and his successor's prime attempt was to make China (now inhabited by more than 700 million people) into a first-rate industrial and even financial power. Now they would tolerate this or that, but not political opposition. In 1989, a large throng of students demonstrated against the government in a big square in Peking, but they were broken up by a brutal police.

Neither India nor Japan turned Communist. In both of these great countries, the attractions of Communism and consequently the influence of a Communist Party were very small. In India, memories of the relative benevolence of erstwhile British rule and its benefits were a great, if often unacknowledged, asset. The British, too (unlike the French or even the Dutch), decided to accept Indian independence very early after the Second World War. They left in early 1947. The intelligent and opportunist Indian political leader, Jawaharlal Nehru, assisted in the transition. Amazingly, the more than 500 different Indian principalities and their maharajah rulers went along. But large portions of the northeastern and far eastern portions of the Indian Peninsula were inhabited not by Hindus, but by Muslims. Fortunately, both Nehru and the Muslim leader, Muhammad Ali Jinnah, saw that their coexistence within an Indian state was not possible. Hence, the partial partition of the great peninsula of India: on one side, Pakistan, a Muslim state in the northeast; on the other side, Bangladesh, a smaller Muslim enclave in the southeast, one thousand miles away. The partition led to the migration and displacement of millions of people and to the death of tens of thousands. But a solution it was, though imperfect. For decades, India and Pakistan quarreled and even fought along their borders, especially in Kashmir, with its mixed (and largely Muslim) population. In 1962, India faced a mini-war with China, whose troops penetrated beyond India's state borders.

India and Pakistan engaged in more than one mini-war in the 1960s. Later, Bangladesh proclaimed its independence—a great loss for Pakistan. India's own internal troubles were serious. In most cases, they involved language, since there are considerable portions of India where the languages spoken, though not entirely dissimilar, are different from Hindi. From time to time, mutinies, provincial revolts, murderous riots and movements on behalf of separation or autonomy shook the subcontinent, compromising its unity. Yet the democratic and increasingly populist practice of elections kept it from breaking up. The gradual improvement in the living standards of its ever-increasing population helped. In 1966, Indira Gandhi (Nehru's daughter) was elected prime minister. She reigned for ten years and was elected again in 1980; four years later, she was assassinated. She had remarkable ruling talents, but demonstrated an increasing tendency to govern by decree. Her son, Rajiv, assumed the premiership from 1984 to 1990. The Cold War and the historical twentieth century had ended, while electoral democracy in India kept on. "Pourvu que cela dure!"—"Let's hope it lasts!" (as Letitia Bonaparte said whenever she heard of her son Napoleon's successes).

The greatest and most enduring benefit the United States provided the Japanese in 1945 was to allow them to keep their emperor and his advisers and, by and large, their political order. Japan had been very successful well before the Second World War. During the First World War, it had extended its influence and power (one example: in 1917, there was a fleet of Japanese destroyers even in the Mediterranean). After the war, Japan extended its possessions and influence in the western Pacific and in China. The British thought they had to choose: between the United States and Japan. Of course, they preferred the United States. Both the American and the Japanese navies had to contemplate an eventual war in the Pacific. The Japanese thought they ought to choose: expand against Russia in Siberia; expand, at least indirectly, against America in the western Pacific; or expand in eastern and northern China. Two strong powers, and a very weak one. The Japanese opted to move against China.

The Japanese had had a firm foothold on the Asian continent since 1910—namely, their rule over Korea. In 1931, aware of the financial and other limitations of British and American power, they transformed Chinese Manchuria (Manchukuo) into a Japanese satellite state. The next year, they advanced farther south. By 1937, a full-scale Chinese-Japanese war was going on. By 1939, China had been driven from the entire China Sea, which had essentially become a Japanese sea. A year after the Second World War began in Europe, Japan joined a tripartite alliance with Germany and Italy. Britain and the United States supported China. By 1940, Japan had a formidable army and navy, singular throughout the Far East and Asia. It had built the largest battleship in the world. Japan's modern armaments were astonishing, in a country whose steel production was a fraction of that of the United States. (Among other things, Japan built a superb fighter plane, the Zero.) Throughout 1941, Japan and the United States edged closer and closer to war. The course of the war we know:

the end of their negotiations; Pearl Harbor; six months of unbroken Japanese triumphs; then America's piecemeal grinding down of Japan.

Much of Tokyo had been bombed into smithereens; Hiroshima and Nagasaki were destroyed by American atomic bombs; Russia declared war on Japan near the end; Japan gave up all of her conquests in the Far East, including Korea. Yet the country and its people recovered very fast. (This included their memories. They accepted, easily, America's victory and its occupation of Japan; but they did not apologize for their aggressive record before the war.) The Korean War, 1950–1953, was a boon to Japan because of America's strategic and other dependence on its enemy-turned-ally. What followed was the persistence of political stability, together with a spectacular growth of material prosperity, unbroken except for a few years in the 1970s. By 1989, the end of the historical century, average income per person in Japan was slightly higher than that in the United States. The Japanese began to increase their armed forces (the minimal expenditure on these had been one element in their successful budgets); and there were some signs of conflict with China, though not many. Still, the relations between Japan and China may be one of the open questions—if not the main question—of the twenty-first century. On the Asian mainland, a strange remnant of the recent past was the Communist dictatorship of North Korea—that, too, a problem for China as well as for Japan.

South of China and southwest of Japan, Indochina was not spared by the Cold War. It had been a fairly prosperous colony of France since the late nineteenth century; it was then occupied by the Japanese during the Second World War, at the end of which they turned over part of it (Vietnam) to the nationalist Communist chieftain Ho Chi Minh. The French attempted to reestablish their authority in the years after the war, with partial success in the Laotian and Cambodian parts of Indochina, but they met their match with Ho Chi Minh and his guerrilla generals, who defeated them at Dien Bien Phu in 1954. Believing in the "domino" theory—according to which the fall of any country to Communists would inevitably lead to the fall of its neighbors—the United States began to send troops to South Vietnam. By 1964, an entire American army was stationed there. President Lyndon Johnson, remembering American isolationism, wanted to win that war. But he failed. The North Vietnamese were not beaten; an armistice followed. By 1975, all of former Indochina, North and South Vietnam, Cambodia, and Laos were under Communist rule, though not entirely united. Next to and south of them, the dominos did not fall. Thailand and Malaysia were not Communist. In the latter, the British, perhaps for the last time, won a difficult military victory over Communists and guerrillas; then they left the country. The result was an independent Malaysia and, south of it, another city-state, Singapore. By the end of the Cold War, American and Vietnamese relations were approaching normal.

The southernmost continents of the world, Australia and New Zealand, were brave and resolute members of the British Empire in both world wars. Their soldiers and seamen (and, on occasion, their generals) gave great and, at times, decisive help to their mother country. They were not directly threatened by an enemy power until 1942, when the Japanese approached northwestern Australia; but that danger faded quickly, mostly because of the presence of American naval power. After the war, and during the rest of the century, Australia's main concern was immigration to a continent still largely empty. The prospect that large numbers of Asians and other nonwhites would move to Australia or New Zealand did not materialize. The democratic stability and prosperity of the Antipodes continued throughout the Cold War, in which—unlike their involvement in the two world wars —their participation was small.

———————

During the twentieth century (more precisely: after the Second World War), the most radical and ominous changes in the political, social, and racial geography of the globe happened in Africa. This enormous continent lay beyond the range of the two world wars, except in the north, where, during the Second World War, British, German, and Italian armies fought in Libya and westernmost Egypt, and for a short time Americans fought in Algeria and Tunisia. As late as 1940, almost all of Africa was still colonized by European powers: France, Britain, Belgium, Portugal, Italy, Spain (the Union of South Africa was a self-governing part of the British Commonwealth). Egypt was something of a British protectorate. The colonization of Africa had been relatively recent; most of it had occurred during the latter half of the nineteenth century. We have seen that at the beginning of the twentieth century, there were only two independent or noncolonial states in Africa: Liberia in the west (founded by former African-American slaves) and Abyssinia in the east. At the end of the Second World War, the political geography of Africa had not yet changed. But soon, the white powers' colonies would vanish. They were succeeded, almost everywhere, by murderous chaos.

The French colonies in North Africa differed from the rest. France had occupied and settled Algiers as early as 1830; and Tunisia, fifty years later. By the twentieth century, there were about one million Frenchmen (as well as Italians and Spaniards) living in Algeria, the only substantial presence of white people in

Africa, except for those of Dutch and British origin in the far south of the continent. The French, after the Second World War, were determined to keep these lands and their people as part of France. After fifteen years of struggle, they gave up. The one million Frenchmen abandoned what to many of them were ancestral lands, withdrawing to France with bitterness in their hearts. Even General de Gaulle, who in 1958 resumed his French presidency and attempted to keep a French presence in Algeria, saw that this was no longer possible. He recognized the independence of Algeria in 1962. Tunisia and French Morocco had achieved that six years earlier. In the long Algerian War, at least half a million people died. There was a bloody civil war in Algeria in the early 1990s. But what was once French North Africa was often spared the barbarism and chaos that afflicted most of Africa, partly because of the French-educated leaders of their early independence.

In 1960, Belgium and Britain (and France south and west of the Sahara) gave up their colonies; Portugal followed about fourteen years later. Immediately, about thirty "states" in Africa declared their independence, their sovereignty, and their new borders. Many of these entities were set up along artificial geographic lines. By 1990, there were about fifty such states, including some islands close to Africa in the Indian Ocean, soon members of the United Nations. Some of these "states" fought short wars with one another. Almost all of them became involved in civil wars that, in most cases, were tribal conflicts during and after which hundreds of thousands of people were killed. Much of this began immediately after "independence"—for example, in the former Belgian Congo, ravaged by a barbaric civil (more precisely: noncivil) war between successive tribal leaders. To sum up or even to list these wars and mass murders in Africa would call for perhaps dozens of pages. To state that after 1960 most of Africa descended into or was marked by chaos is not an exaggeration. Most of the new African "states" were now ruled by dictators and tyrants, all of them having gained power through crude military murders for which the classic term "coups d'état" is inadequate. The title and the theme of Joseph Conrad's *Heart of Darkness,* written in the nineteenth century, was applicable to much of Africa a century later.

Here and there in the 1970s, the Soviet Union supported such tyrannies, taking advantage of the declarations by some of these dictators (in Abyssinia, for example) that they were "Marxists." This did not last long. More regrettable was the American policy under Reagan to sustain and support any African regime that declared itself anti-Communist. (By way of example: in 1981 or 1982, this president received the tyrant Samuel Doe, ruler of Liberia, in the White House—the same man who had been seen to preside over a spectacle in which his soldiers, having defeated and captured one of the regime's opponents, ate portions of his body, still warm. Two years later, in another ceremony, the next ruler, Charles Taylor, cut off and ate an ear of his rival.)

The only areas of Africa where considerable portions of white people still remained were Rhodesia and South Africa. In the former, whites put up strong resistance against black majority rule, but that lasted only for a few years; after a while, Rhodesia became Zimbabwe. In the former Union of South Africa, whites and "coloreds" (men and women of mixed race) represented about 30 percent of the population; the original Dutch and British people kept up their "apartheid" (separation of the races), which was enforced by legislation that had been passed after the Second World War—but the system of segregation was ultimately dissolved without civil war. A remarkable man, without

whom a compromise was hardly possible, was Nelson Mandela—
a black leader who, after a quarter-century in prison, joined the
South African president, F. W. de Klerk, in an agreement to abol-
ish apartheid and accept majority rule in South Africa. This happened in and after 1989, when the historical twentieth century
was over.

What Mandela's successors did, and would do, does not belong within the province of this book. But perhaps what fits here
are two sentences of historical speculation. At the end of the
twentieth century in Africa, as well as in the Middle East, only
two places remained with a considerable white population: South
Africa, at the southern tip of that vast continent; and the State of
Israel, thousands of miles away, on the western shores of Asia.
Will they remain so another hundred years from now?

———————

Last but not least, I must turn to Latin America in the twentieth
century. "South and Central America" would be a more proper
designation; or "Latino America"—less precise, but telling. It is
another vast continent, of almost seven million square miles.
Spanish and Portuguese explorers had mapped it and begun settling there even before they did so in North America. Unlike the
latter, Latin America did not see very large numbers of set-
tlers coming from the Old World. It is astonishing that, by and
large, through five somnolent and raw centuries, the growing
and considerably mixed populations of South and Central America maintained their predominantly Roman Catholic religion, as
well as their Spanish and Portuguese languages. The examples of
the French and American revolutions affected, somewhat belat-
edly, a few men of their small ruling classes after 1815. The result
was a series of wars of independence against a weak Spain—in-

dependence that was achieved in a few years. In 1867, Mexico revolted against the brief rule of a European emperor. Brazil, also independent, kept its Portuguese-born emperor until 1889. Cuba revolted against Spain a few years later, and achieved semi-independence in 1898 with American armed support. During the First World War, Brazil sent a small army to fight with the Americans and the British in Europe. Between the wars, the British presence and influence in South America gave way to those of the Americans. In the Second World War, Argentina was neutral; in October 1945 (again, oddly, after Germany had been defeated), General Juan Perón, who evinced considerable pro-German sympathy, assumed power there for a dozen years. But dependence on the United States was still a primary factor, especially in South America. In Central America, sentiments and politics tended to be different. In Mexico, a radically anti-Catholic and anti-American political party ruled during the late 1920s and 1930s, attempting to expropriate, among other things, American oil properties there; fortunately, there was no armed conflict between Mexico and the United States (except for a few marginal incursions along their border during the First World War). Mexico's frequent political chaos settled down before 1939. The cities of Latin America grew enormously. By the end of the twentieth century, Mexico City had 19 million people, Rio de Janeiro had 10 million, Buenos Aires had 11 million—while large numbers of indigenous rural folk (as well as many people in the urban conglomerations) were still very poor.

The nineteenth and twentieth centuries saw few wars among the states of Latin America. There were none in South America, and only two ridiculous mini-wars between Central American states (Honduras versus Nicaragua, and Honduras versus El Salvador, the latter because of a football match). But the Cold War did involve a few Latin American states—or rather, their ambitious leaders. No matter what they proclaimed, an essential sentiment involved was not so much antagonism between Capitalism and Communism as it was anti-Americanism. The American government and the Central Intelligence Agency were inclined to think otherwise: they worried about the danger of Communism and Soviet support for these states and leaders. There was some evidence for the latter, but not much. Thus, the CIA, with some other help from Central American states, overthrew Guatemala's ruler in 1954, and helped to depose and kill the freely elected Chilean prime minister, Salvador Allende, in 1973. More serious, of course, was the problem of Cuba. Its dictator, Batista, was conquered by the former guerrilla leader Fidel Castro in 1959. Castro now sought support from the Soviet Union, more than half a world away. We have seen how all of this developed into a dangerous crisis in Soviet-American relations: partial and indecisive American attempts to overthrow Castro with American help; frantic efforts by Castro to obtain support from the Russians; the decision of the latter to ship Russian defensive missiles to Cuba in 1962; the sudden withdrawal of the Russians. Castro lived on, physically and mentally ailing. The United States prudently chose not to invade Cuba. (It sent troops to Cuba's neighbor, the Dominican Republic, in 1965; to the tiny Caribbean island of Grenada in 1983; and to Panama in 1989.)

A strange, episodic war occurred in 1982. The president of Argentina, Leopoldo Galtieri, a military man, decided—probably to enhance his nationalist and populist support—to invade and occupy the Falkland Islands, a lone British property in the South Atlantic, occasionally claimed by Argentina. The British responded; one or two warships were sunk; they reoccupied the Falklands in a month. Galtieri was gone. Argentine populism and nationalism were not.

Throughout the second half of the twentieth century, many or even most of the Latin American states were ruled by military dictatorships. In 1989, Panama's dictator, Manuel Noriega, was a ludicrous example of the worst of them. He was a drug dealer on a large scale. In late December 1989, he declared war against the United States. American Marines entered Panama, overthrowing him in ten days. At first, he took refuge in the Vatican Legation; the American forces played ear-shattering rock music nearby to unhinge him, which was not difficult. Noriega gave up in three days, whereupon he was taken to Florida for trial and sentenced to forty years in prison. All of this took place in the last few days of 1989, the end of the Cold War, and the end of the historical twentieth century.

———

Some—if not most—readers of the foregoing pages may have been either impressed or startled by my ironic or even sarcastic dismissal of the deplorable, dwarfish dictatorships in the so-called Third World. Their rulers did matter, and they will continue to matter. But that word "dismissal" is not quite correct. What concerns me, and what ought to concern me, are the subjects of those rulers. We in Western Europe or North America should not claim that our traditions are naturally and perhaps irrevocably superior to those of the peoples of Africa, the Middle East, or Central and South America. "Democracy," more than "rule"—the equality of human beings—is advancing, whether we are conscious of it or not. I believe that this is God's design. I do not expect all of my readers to see it so. Still, I expect most of them to recognize that the democratization of the world has been taking place and that it is some kind of advance rather than a retreat. Populism and nationalism are the very worst (and, alas, powerful) components of democracy. Whether they will overwhelm it forever I cannot tell. What I am compelled to say is that even the most miserable and corrupted peoples of the Third World are our brothers and sisters.

Democracy inspires many people to move. The movement of poorer people to more prosperous parts of the world has been increasing, especially since the 1960s. This has affected many Western and Southern European countries, but especially the United States, where immigrants, mostly from Mexico, by 1990 became 25 or even 30 percent of the population of California and Texas. Much of this immigration has been illegal. Because of the geographic conditions, to halt or even control it has been very difficult. Until recently, the assimilation and integration of children of all kinds of immigrants in the United States have been successful. Whether this will prevail or not, no one can tell. Whatever may happen with the borders of states—that is, with the political map of the globe—its demographic map is changing and will continue to change. Everything suggests that this movement of peoples will continue in the twenty-first century.

17

THE LIMITATIONS OF HUMAN KNOWLEDGE

A transitional century—Inheritances of the preceding one—
Positive achievements—Technologies—Weakening enthusiasm for some of its applications—Cultural and civilizational
decline—Shortcomings of scientific determinism; scattered
recognitions thereof—We and our earth: again at the center
of the universe

THE TWENTIETH CENTURY WAS A very transitional one. Of
course, so is every century, between two others—but the twentieth century was transitional, too, between two great ages: between the so-called Modern Age and what is coming after it.
Something similar had happened in the sixteenth and seven-
teenth centuries: the transition from the Middle Ages to the
Modern Age—even though as late as 1700 these designations
(especially the latter one) did not exist. Again, it will take a long
time before an adjective, a name, will be affixed to the age now
current. To speculate about this is senseless.

Whether in the life of a single human being or in the lives
of entire countries, let alone continents, history is never of one
piece. Still, we may essay some generalizations about the great
changes that took place during the century now past, since

(in various ways) they have affected great varieties of peoples throughout the globe. To begin with, the average life span of human beings increased. Some age-old diseases were radically contained or even eliminated. More children attended school than at any earlier time in history. One amazing global development has been the increasing universality of English as a second language. A previously unimaginable burgeoning of communications and then an even less imaginable mass of information have become available to billions of people. Famines, recorded or unrecorded, were rarer than at almost any time in the past. Some of the twentieth century's famines were manmade, a result of dictatorships or social turmoil. Likewise human-caused were the millions of deaths due to wars, civil wars, revolutions, persecutions, and liquidations between 1914 and 1989. Much of all of this was made possible by advanced technologies. Some of the technological feats of the twentieth century surpassed just about all projections made as recently as a century ago—including achievements such as sending humans into space and enabling them to walk on the surface of the moon. Of course, there has also been skepticism about the technologizing of the world—a topic to which we shall return.

Billions of people, probably at least half of the population of the globe, were materially better off in 1989 than their forebears had been in 1914. Whether they were happier than their ancestors, no one can tell; indeed, no one should be allowed even to speculate about this—not historians, not sociologists, not psychoanalysts, not nutrition or hormone experts, not even the most sensitive thinkers and writers of our (or their) times.

A century does not start (or end) suddenly. In many ways, life in the nineteenth century—its material circumstances and, perhaps even more, its habits of mind—seeped into the twentieth century and stayed with it for a long time. One of the most important of these ongoing movements was the democratization of the world. Social differences became liquefied—indeed, almost to the point of vanishing. Almost everywhere, the influence and even the presence of the more or less traditional aristocracies disappeared. Of course, extremes of wealth and poverty existed even in the most advanced democracies, but social "classes" were relevant to the lives of ever fewer people. What became more and more acceptable—and unquestionable—was the idea of democracy or, more precisely, of popular sovereignty. To most people, the latter meant the attractions of populism and nationalism. Few people understood that populism was not liberalism and that nationalism was different from patriotism.

The parallel ideas of democracy and liberalism belonged to the nineteenth century, and continued into the twentieth. But the ideas and the practices of Western European, British, and even American liberal democracy became unpopular in most European (not to speak of Latin American) states soon after the First World War. One shattering example of this was the rise of Hitler—and, before him, Mussolini—with their widespread popularity in Europe; it took a Second World War to bring an end to them and their rule. But the victory of Churchillian Britain, Rooseveltian America, and of course of Stalinist Russia did not mean a resurrection of the nineteenth-century ideals and practices of liberal democracy. Well before the end of the twentieth century, "liberal" often became an unpopular adjective, in the United States and in other, now-traditional democracies (and after 1989, in most states in Eastern Europe). Well before the end of the twentieth century, the classic political adjectives "liberal" and "conservative" lost much of their meaning, even though these words—especially the latter—began to be used inaccurately among most "antiliberal" people. (By that time, Marxism and Communism were dead.)

There is profound wisdom in what Wendell Berry wrote: "Instead of 'liberal' and 'conservative,' or Leftist and Rightist divisions among people, a new division is taking place: between people who think of themselves as machines and people who think of themselves as creatures."[1]

Consider, too, what Tocqueville wrote 180 years ago in the second—and infrequently read—volume of his *Democracy in America* (here translated by Henry Reeve):

> Because the civilization of ancient Rome perished in consequence of the invasion of Barbarians, we are perhaps too apt to think that civilization cannot perish in any other manner. If the light by which we are guided is ever extinguished, it will dwindle by degrees and expire of itself. By dint of close adherence to mere applications, principles would be lost sight of; and when the principles were wholly forgotten, the methods derived from them would be ill pursued. New methods could no longer be invented, and men would continue, without intelligence and without art, to apply scientific processes no longer understood.

Or the stunning prophecy that the great Jacob Burckhardt made 150 years ago: "The sudden change from democracy will no longer result in the rule of an individual, but in the rule of a mili-

---

1. Compare this with the words of Goebbels printed in the journal *Deutsche Technik* in February 1939: "The bourgeois were alien and hostile to technology; skeptics believed that the roots of the collapse of European culture lay in it. National Socialism has understood how to take the soulless framework of technology and fill it with the rhythm and hot impulses of our time."

tary corporation. And by it, methods will perhaps be used for which even the most terrible despot would not have the heart." Technical methods, unknown by the democratic peoples in whose name these increasingly impersonal means of warfare are employed. After the end of the American Century, a major problem is not so much the existence of American omnipotence as it is the way millions of Americans and many of their politicians unthinkingly believe in it.

Still, history is never of one piece. I will end this short book by mentioning the first signs that people are beginning to have doubts about technology—doubts that are often hardly conscious in their minds as yet, but that certainly exist. At the very beginning of this book I suggested that, perhaps especially in ages of democracy, the most decisive matters involve not material but mental conditions: what and how people think. During the twentieth century, many signs about this were not encouraging. "Culture" and "civilization" are difficult—nay, impossible—to define or even to separate from each other. Yet the standards (and fashions) of culture and civilization have declined to such levels that we may eventually see some kind of reaction to that.

All this is speculation; but what may be culled from the extant record of a now-past century is not. One bit of evidence is found in the arts. Artists, it is often said, are the antennae of the race, but even the most sensitive antenna is not an entirely independent instrument, divorced from context and atmosphere. Compared to the works of earlier centuries, new styles of architecture, painting, literature, and music have been ephemeral, most of them leading nowhere. Of course, there were exceptions, a few faint lights in a manmade universe of glassy darkness.

Yet we may also detect the first signs of waning enthusiasm

where there was once boundless respect for technology. At the end of the nineteenth century, there were countless books, articles, and other manifestations of unbounded optimism about the technological future, breathlessly prophesying many of its benefits. At the end of the twentieth century, we can detect almost nothing like that.

I am a historian, not a prophet. So I will close this book by mentioning, briefly, that during the twentieth century (and here and there even earlier) the first signs of a new tendency of thinking were beginning to appear. Significant evidence of this is the fact that more and more people are aware of the catastrophes that can result from technology, ranging from nuclear explosions to genetic manipulations. Another, less widely recognized element is that people are acknowledging the shortcomings of scientific determinism—its dependence on mechanical causality (which, as Aristotle noted, is but one of the multiple types of human causality); its adherence to the unwarranted belief that the same causes necessarily result in the same effects; its unwillingness to understand and actually see that the human mind interferes with and alters these very causalities.

Initial evidence of such awareness has been apparent in spheres ranging from fine arts to physics—in the recognition that humans participate through the very act of seeing; in the chastened realization that our very knowledge of matter is but the result of our participation in the material universe by our observations. An early example of this is the work of the Impressionist painters, whose art depended on participation. "Reality" may be external, but it depends entirely on what the painter sees. An Impressionist painting suggests this; the painter must illustrate ("lustrate"), in the original sense of that verb, how and what we see. So Impressionism was a symptom not of decadence, but of a rise of consciousness. Of course, these painters did not know the *historical* meaning of this, but their Impressionist approach preceded quantum physics by about a half-century. (After that, in the twentieth century, came movements such as cubism and other abstract forms in art, and string theory in physics. The degeneration was awful, but it will not last.)

Then, in the 1920s ("the only modern decade," as I said earlier), came profound advances in the study of matter itself. In research on atomic fission and the nature of the subatomic world, great physicists such as Werner Heisenberg and Niels Bohr formulated what has become known as the Uncertainty Principle, meaning that what we can know and see about atomic particles is inseparable from, and altered by, our interference in their "observation"—the knower cannot be separated from the known. And within this is a greater and deeper meaning: that we, on our little, warm planet, are (again? anew?) at the very center of the universe. The universe was, and is, not our creation. But we human beings on this earth have invented it, and go on inventing it from time to time.

That this recognition came about during the 1900s ought to be listed as one of that century's most important achievements—even though few people, including most physicists, are aware of its significance. No matter: it will bring forth all kinds of results. It would be wrong to name it a new humanism, since the old humanism arose from the belief that the limits of human knowledge and of its applications were potentially boundless. Our twentieth-century recognitions, no matter how scattered and still hardly conscious, must, and will, issue not from human arrogance but from human humility. Perhaps just as important as our recognition of our central situation in the universe is our recognition that the limitations of our human knowledge do not restrict but enrich us.

INDEX

INDEX

Cold War *(continued)*
victory in, 164; Australia and New
Zealand in, 198; Berlin blockade,
155; Communist victory in China
and, 192; Cuban Missile Crisis and,
163; end of, 172, 174, 177, 181–183, 191,
194, 204; Europe as main theater of,
146; Latin America and, 203; Middle East and, 186; origins of, 142,
187–188; Soviet retreat and, 179–181;
Stalin and, 176; West European
Communist parties and, 149. *See
also* "Iron curtain"
Colombia, 68, 71
Colonialism, 10, 73, 177. *See also* Anticolonialism
Columbus, Christopher, 67
Commonwealth, British, 72, 133, 185,
198
Communism, 2, 8, 90, 96, 98, 203; anticolonialism and, 38; attempted
spread of, after First World War, 35–
36; Capitalism in worldwide struggle with, 84; Castro's embrace of,
162; Cold War and, 11; death of, 209;
fellow travelers of, 169–170; in Germany after First World War, 41, 79;
Great Depression and, 88; in
Greece, 141, 149; imposed on Eastern Europe, 61; in Indochina, 196–
197; from internationalism to nationalism, 27, 47; in Italy, 81; as more
radical version of Socialism, 85; in
Poland, 179; revolution in Russia
(1917), 2, 24–26; in United States,

64; working-class indifference to,
45. *See also* Bolsheviks; Soviet
Union
Communist Manifesto (Marx and En-
gels), 45
Congo, Belgian, 199
Conservatism, 10, 63, 170–171, 208;
anti-Communism and, 170, 172; as
nineteenth-century ideology, 14
Conservative Party, British, 113, 115,
116
Coolidge, Calvin, 58
Coral Sea, battle of the, 132
Cossacks, 45, 73
Coughlin, Father Charles, 88
Credit, economic role of, 87
Croatia, 33
Cuba, 11, 70, 71; Castro's revolution,
161–162, 203; independence from
Spain, 202; missile crisis, 161–163
Czechoslovakia, 33, 148, 177; Commu-
nist regime installed in, 150; Czech
national socialists, 42; end of Com-
munist rule in, 181; French alliance
with, 35; German-speaking Austri-
ans in, 42; Hitler's conquest of, 103–
104; Warsaw Pact invasion of, 179

Daladier, Edouard, 104
Deflation, 87
De Gaulle, Charles, 8, 141, 155; Alge-
rian War and, 199; as leader of Free
France, 130, 139, 148
De Klerk, F. W., 201
Democracy, 11, 55, 56, 179; advance